New Selected Poems

JOHN MATTHIAS was born in 1941 in Columbus, Ohio. He has been a Visiting Fellow in poetry at Clare Hall, Cambridge, and lived for much of the 70s and 80s in East Anglia. He teaches at the University of Notre Dame. Matthias's recent books include *A Gathering of Ways* (1991), *Swimming at Midnight: Selected Shorter Poems* (1995), *Beltane at Aphelion: Longer Poems* (1995), and *Pages: New Poems and Cuttings* (2000). In 1998 Robert Archambeau edited *Word Play Place: Essays on the Poetry of John Matthias*.

Also by John Matthias

Poetry
  Bucyrus (1970)
  Turns (1975)
  Crossing (1979)
  Bathory & Lermontov (1980)
  Northern Summer (1984)
  A Gathering of Ways (1991)
  Swimming at Midnight (1995)
  Beltane at Aphelion (1995)
  Pages: New Poems & Cuttings (2000)
  Working Progress, Working Title (2002)
  Swell & Variations on the Song of Songs (2003)

Translations
  Contemporary Swedish Poetry (1980)
    (with Göran Printz-Påhlson)
  Jan Östergren: Rainmaker (1983)
    (with Göran Printz-Påhlson)
  The Battle of Kosovo (1987)
    (with Vladeta Vuckovic)
  Three-Toed Gull: Selected Poems of Jesper Svenbro (2003)
    (with Lars-Håkan Svensson)

Editions
  23 Modern British Poets (1971)
  Introducing David Jones (1980)
  David Jones: Man and Poet (1989)
  Selected Works of David Jones (1992)

Criticism
  Reading Old Friends (1992)

New Selected Poems

JOHN MATTHIAS

CAMBRIDGE

PUBLISHED BY SALT PUBLISHING
PO Box 937, Great Wilbraham, Cambridge PDO CB1 5JX United Kingdom
PO Box 202, Applecross, Western Australia 6153

First published 2004

Printed and bound in the United Kingdom by Lightning Source

Typeset in Swift 9.5 / 13

ISBN 1 84471 040 8 paperback

SP

1 3 5 7 9 8 6 4 2

To my students at the University of Notre Dame
1967–2004

" . . . *there in the interstices*"

Contents

Acknowledgments

Many of the poems in this selection first appeared in books published by Swallow Press in the US and Anvil Press in the UK. I am grateful to David Sanders, director of Swallow Press / Ohio University Press and to Peter Jay, publisher of Anvil Press, for permission to reprint poems that originally appeared in the following books: *Bucyrus* (1970), *Turns* (1975), *Crossing* (1979), *Northern Summer* (1984), *A Gathering of Ways* (1991), *Swimming at Midnight* (1995), *Beltane at Aphelion* (1995), and *Pages: New Poems & Cuttings* (2000). All of these books were published by Swallow; *Turns*, *Crossing* and *Northern Summer* were co-published by Anvil. New poems appearing in this book have been published in *PN Review*, *Samizdat*, *Ars-Interpres*, and the Momotombito chapbook series. I would also like to thank the editors of those magazines which have published my poems regularly in the past and in which most of the pieces in this book first appeared in journal form from 1970 to the present: *TriQuarterly*, *Poetry*, *Salmagundi*, *PN Review*, *Chicago Review*, *Parnassus*, *Another Chicago Magazine*, and *Boundary 2*.

I would particularly like to thank Michael Anania, Robert Archambeau, Joe Francis Doerr, Kevin Ducey, John Peck, Vincent Sherry, Mike Smith, and James Walton for their support and close reading during various periods when the poems in this book were being written and throughout the difficult year when the selections were made. My special thanks to Bridget Brown for preparing the manuscript, and to John Kinsella and Chris Hamilton-Emery for their enthusiasm for the entire project. It is always a pleasure to work with the team at Salt. Finally, my thanks to Douglas Kinsey, whose painting reproduced on the cover has hung in my living room for more than twenty-five years.

Part I

Swimming at Midnight

*[Near my grandparents' home at the outskirts of town, a stone
quarry was established, then abandoned, nearly a hundred and fifty years
ago. The early blasting hit water, and after many soundings were taken, the
management concluded that they had uncovered a bottomless lake, fed, they
surmised, by a sizeable underground river.]*

Under a pine and confusion:
ah! Tangles of clothes: (come
on, silly, nobody's here:) and
naked as fish, a boy and a girl.
(Nobody comes here: nobody looks:
nobody watches us watching us
watch.) Except the police.
Thighs slide into the moon.
Humbly, into the stars: Mirrored,
flashes a father's red eye, a
blue-bitten mother's red lip: No
Swimming Allowed In The Quarry
At Night. (Anyway, nevertheless
and moreover: feel how warm!) here,
among the reflections. (Feel the
water's mouth and its hands, feel
them imitate mine: can there truly
be any danger?) danger allowed in
the quarry at night? can people
really have drowned? (Now my body
is only water alive, and aeons
ago you were a fish growing
legs —) well, dust to dust, a
curious notion. But quarry water on
dust green with seed! Quarry water
forbidden on land after dark! What
young forms of vegetation emerge.
What new colors of light.

Diptych

I

Carpet flames.
Chain grip: incense
in a cup. Violins
and mandolins re-
corded. Oddly off.
Stumble dancer,
rafter slanting down.
(What is now beyond
you now my dear?)
Hold it (having
hardened) with a kiss.
He had lied
for years.

II

Zero on ice.
Tire spun: smoke
to three a.m. Hail
and also headlight
dimming. Oddly out.
Weep then weeper,
headlight out and hail.
(Who is now beside
me now and dear?)
Break it (having
buckled) with a fist.
She had cried
for years.

Arzeno Kirkpatrick

Should he, if the telephone rings,
pick it up? And if a knock should
come at the door? He ponders, Arzeno
Kirkpatrick, the questions. Another
occurs: what if a light should
suddenly flash in the yard?
It is late; Arzeno Kirkpatrick
is tired. He sips his tea and
smokes his cigarettes. He
ponders, Arzeno Kirkpatrick,
the questions.

There is a light in the yard.
The telephone rings.
There is an angry knocking at the door.

Renaissance

The knocked-up look is back!
(old accurate Van Eyck):
the turned-up pointed shoes,
the twin-peaked cap.
Gentlemen, there's no one
here but Gentlemen.

And Ladies.

And the Court.

Virgins of St. Denis
bare their privies for
the prince. And I am priest
and altar, consecrated host.
Bread and whiskey on
my loins, a wooden
phallus, nails:
I stiffen and endure.

Empty out the coffins, then.

Disinter the bones.

An Absence

I

Korok.

And of Korok, Kazi or Brelum
Teka or Tecta.

Libushka. Libushka
of Korok, a sybil.

Weleska said: our lady
Libushka is dead.

But let us continue to rule.

II

The tithes were refused.
The clergymen were assaulted.
Henry IV deferred to
The Bishop of Bremen.

Excommunicate (about '97)
And damned, the men
Of that region deferred
To the women.

III

"Hordes of devils are making for France!"
("The French, you know, are
a restless and turbulent people.")
Run the country in absence
Of Husband and Son?
Libushka of Korok, a sybil.

IV

A toad the size of a goose or a duck.
The rhetoric of crusades.

Statement

Once upon a time Ezra Pound, when he was still a young man, not so young he was still an Imagist, but still young enough that he was a Vorticist, once upon a time ol' Ez had him a friend called Gaudier-Brzeska. Now this Gaudier, this Gaudier-Brzeska who was a friend of Ezra Pound's (Pound the Vorticist—always honoring craft) this Gaudier was a craftsman of genius—a sculptor. He worked on stone with his hands, and his hands were trained— *trained* hands. I mean the man knew what he did, didn't hack it with cudgels and hammers, didn't just kick it or punch it, he *sculpted* the stone with his exquisite perfectly trained controlled and controlling hands. (If, for example, the man had liked violin, he would have taken the time to find out where one puts down one's fingers. If, for example, the man had liked the cooking of pastries, he would have learned from a pastry cook how to cook pastries. If, for example, the man had liked carpentry, he would have learned that screws hold under certain kinds of stresses where nails don't—etc. etc.) But his medium was stone. And he was a craftsman of genius—*of genius*. He had learned his craft, do you follow me? And that turned out (it does turn out, if you're serious, but most people aren't) to spell the difference between freedom and slavery, or, to be more precise in the parable, between freedom and imprisonment. "The instincts are not free springs of connation towards a goal. They are, so far as they can be abstractly separated, unconscious necessities, as Kant realized. They are unfree. But in their realization as behaviour, when these innate things-in-themselves become things-for-themselves and interact with their environment (which also changes and is not the dead world of physics) they also change. Above all, they are changed in human culture. As a result of this change, these necessities become conscious, become emotion and thought; they exist for themselves and are altered thereby. The change *is* the emotion or thought, and now they are no longer the instincts, for they are conscious and consciousness is not an ethereal but a material determining relationship. The necessity that is conscious is not the necessity that is unconscious. The conscious goal is different from the blind instinctive goal. It is freer." So then Gaudier. Gaudier choosing craft and consciousness, choosing freedom. So then Gaudier— Gaudier refusing to be enslaved by refusing to know, Gaudier refusing imprisonment. But they tried, the governments and their jailers, they tried, the governments and jailers unconscious and therefore unfree, to jail, in the war, this conscious spirit, this Gaudier. But Gaudier loved freedom, and because he loved freedom learned craft. Because he loved freedom learned craft so perfectly that he became a craftsman of genius. And his medium was stone. Stone were the jails of the governments and the jailers. Stone was his medium—a genius with exquisite perfectly trained controlled and controlling hands. Free hands. Free because they knew craft. Jails, Penitentiaries, Sanatoriums, all made out of stone. Stone walls, many feet thick. Stone jails. Jail-thick stone walls where they put him, craftsman and free, they—the governments making their wars.

Minutes after they threw him there in his cell, minutes after they locked him in that cage of stone, Gaudier, Pound's friend the Vorticist, took, with his bare hands, and eight-foot-thick wall apart and went home.

Five Lyrics from "Poem in Three Parts"

I

Sing-bonga, angered
by the smoke, sent
crows. Later he slept
in the furnace.

Sing-anga, earlier
and far away, a
fetus found and
burned:
      "on that ash
        erect a temple, Yakut shaman."

Yang & Yin
Yin & Yang

For the smith
and his bride,
these coals.

II

could boil,
melt
    (ego in
      hand)
his world.

therefore feared
as agent
    ("public
      menace")

matter unre-
generate
mirrors
(crime).

Verbum dictum factum: god in
the vowels of the earth:

ascribe unto
these metals,
Hermes,
need.

    III

(otherwise
perceive the imperfection
understand

not to imperfection
even otherwise
command

dross & refuse &
decay

ascend
condense)

Philosophy, he held, was out of hand.

IV

Whether C. was
        duped "per doctrinam"
Whether C. knew
        Shuchirch at all

        William de Brumley, "chaplain lately
dwelling with the Prior of Harmondsworth"—
does he lie?

Whether C. was a
victim or student . . .

                (hermaphroditic rebis
                there appeared.

                Probably not.)

                Probably not.

                later,
                after.

V

The still-providing
world is not
enough: we add.

Ponder matter
where impatient
sleepers wait.

And Aphrodite
saw her soul
was stone.

And Nargajuna
dreamed that
he was glad.

Between

Between here
and away
is a
way

and a point
to be made.

what matter
now
is how?

to leave is
to the point

it is

it is a way,

(and equally
the coffee
and the
calm)

Facts from an Apocryphal Midwest

for Michael Anania and i.m. Ken Smith

1. SEVEN MOVES TOWARD EMBARKATION ON THE LOCAL RIVER

Nous embarquâmes le troisième Decembre
avec trente hommes, dans huit canots

& nous remontâmes la rivière des Miamis
faisant nostre route au Sud . . .
—Fr. Hennepin

～

Overheard on Riverside cycling toward
the bridge and U.S. 31:
Look, he says, *if things had turned out*

differently a long time back,
not just you, but everybody on this
river might be speaking French

& trading otter skins or beaver pelts.

～

1 arpent: *160 pieds de Roi*
84 arpents: say about one league
28 arpents, then, to the mile

But distances are tricky
and it often takes
you longer
than you think.

～

Four thin men, two white, two black
stand fishing near the Farmer's Market
where the Amish come to sell

their vegetables and breads. It's early
afternoon in heavy, muggy August.
The river's low & stagnant for ten miles.

Catchin' anything? Jus' tin cans an' tires
Four thin fishermen—
and no Miamis, not a Potawatami in town.

~

Oui-oui-la-Meche
L'Espérance de la Brie

Père Gabriel
Père Louis
Père Zénobe

Réné Robert Cavelier (Sieur de la Salle)

~

"There were several varieties of league; but the one that
Hennepin undoubtedly meant was the ordinary league of 84
arpents. That will give 3.051 plus 5220-5280th statute miles. You
need to have no hesitation in assuming Hennepin's league to be
3.052 statute or English miles."

"We embarked on the 3rd of December with thirty men in eight
canoes, and ascended the river of the Miamis, taking our course

to the south-east for about twenty five leagues. We could not make out the portage which we were to take with our canoes and all our equipage in order to go and embark at the source of the river Seignelay, and as we had gone higher up in a canoe without discovering the place where we were to march by land to take the other river which runs by the Illinois, we halted to wait for the Sieur de La Salle, who had gone exploring on land; and as he did not return we did not know what course to pursue."

—Fr. Hennepin

2. FIVE MAPS, A MEDICINE BAG, AND A MYTH

≈

Carte de la Nouvelle Découverte

Illuminations of the priests haranguing Indians.
Much conjecture. Crudely drawn Ohio
and Missouri and Wisconsin ...
Père Marquette's route back it's got
entirely wrong.

≈

Carte Généralle de la France Septentrionale

The Ohio's called the *Ouaboustikou*.
Pictures of the creatures
native to the Mississippi's western plains
include a camel, ostriches, giraffes.
A monster seen by Père Marquette and Joliet:

Horns of a deer, beard of a tiger,
face like that of a man—Also
many nasty scales
and a long tail wound around it.

~

Carte de Jean Baptiste Franquelin

La Salle's Starved Rock, a natural fortress
all but inaccessible a hundred feet
above the Illinois, the little colony below.
La Nouvelle France: Penobscot
to the south of Lake Champlain and to
the Mohawk near Schenectady
and then where Susquehanna rises
and the Allegheny past the south of Erie
on to Southern Michigan & then
northwest to the Mississippi tributaries.
La Louisiane: The Mississippi valley,
the Ohio valley, Texas.
Rivière Colbert. Grande Rivière des Emissourittes.
Rivière des Illinois, ou Macopins.
And down below Starved Rock the colony:
Shawnees, Ouiatenons, Miamis,
Piankishaws, Illinois, Kilaticas, & Ouabonas.
3,900 warriors huddling
under *Le Rocher* & trembling for the Iroquois.

~

Carte de M. Mathieu Sâgean

The nation of the Acanibas, towns and castles,
King Hagaren, Montezuma's kin.
Women riding unicorns. Bricks of solid gold.
Caravans of horsemen
and a thousand oxen bearing priceless treasures.
Everyone polygamist.
Perpetual summer there, a cool breeze.

∾

Rand McNally Atlas, 1985

The old Sauk trail, they say
still runs under U.S. 12
north from Niles to Detroit.
U.S. 20 takes it west through
Rolling Prairie to Chicago.

You can drive a car that's named
for Cadillac up to U.S. 12
to Ypsilanti, turning north
at 94 to a port named for the Hurons.
You can even drive
your Pontiac to Pontiac.
But only trickster Wiske's brother
Chibyabos ever drove
in a Tecumseh to Tecumseh.

∾

What's in your medicine bag, Neshnabe?
Gifts from Wiske? Toys?

A skunk's bladder. Ear of a bat.
Three fat joints and a switchblade knife.
Pussy hairs from Mama Chickie's whores.
What's in your map, little Frog?
If I drop this at your feet, it will explode.

∾

The story goes that poor and feeble Tisha had a vision. A stranger dressed elaborately in clothing he had never seen before appeared and said he'd build a boat for him to travel over land and sea and rivers in if Tisha showed him just how big it ought to be. Tisha then took twelve enormous paces, smiled at the solemn stranger, waited. Suddenly a ship appeared the likes of which he'd never seen or even dreamed of. It had thin tree trunks planted vertically upon its decks, it had white sheets attached, it had nine great black guns. Boat-Maker and Tisha climbed aboard and sailed over land and sea and rivers. They met and took aboard a mighty seer, a mighty hearer, a mighty eater, a mighty runner, and a mighty maker of wind. These were Boat-Maker's friends.

One day after many travels they arrived at the camp of evil Matjimanito. He and all his friends were cannibals, and many bones lay all around. Matjimanito challenged Tisha to a contest where he'd gamble for his life. When Boat-Maker saw poor Tisha trembling, he insisted on a game which Matjimanito had never played before. When Tisha shouted *now*, Wind-Maker blew the ship up in the air above the village shouting out: *everybody's bones get out of here!* The nine black cannons fired, the dead all came alive, and Matjimanito and his men all perished when the ship came down and crushed them. After that, Tisha was a famous man. He travelled all the world over with this elegant protector and his friend. Eventually, Boat-Maker taught him how to speak his language. It was French.

3. COPPER, SOUTH FROM LAKE SUPERIOR

... and down the old Sauk trail
although there were then, three and more millennia
before the French, no Sauks ...

The trail itself was there, and those who mined
the copper, *they* were there,
and those who came on urgent journeys from

the lower Mississippi & the Gulf to lug it back
were there, and leaned into
their labors in the mines and on the paths.

Mounds at Moorhouse Parish, at Miamisburg,
tumuli along the northeast
of the marshy lake between the Kankakee and

Portage Prairie with its recent graves & glacial
memories of mastodon & mammoth spit up
needles, chisels, knives & awls in fine profusion—

& when Bernal Diaz entered Tuspan with Cortez,
he found that *every Indian had,
besides his ornaments of gold, a copper axe,*

very highly polished, strangely carved.
The copper came from west and north
of Mackinaw, Sault Ste. Marie, & Whitefish point,

from Minong where ten thousand men once mined
the copper for a thousand years
but left no carvings, writings, signs, nothing

but their simple tools. Their dead they
buried elsewhere. Jacques Marquette was first to put
the island on a white man's map . . .

If the copper came by water to the forest paths,
it came by long canoe along the shores
of Huron into Lake St. Clair and then Detroit

where the trail curved into Canada.
Was Father Claude Allouez, the Jesuit, correct
who said of them who called

themselves *Neshnabek* and the other
tall Algonquins at Green Bay that golden copper
shapes were manitous, that queerly

wrought and efficacious metals were the secret
household gods of Potawatomies
who worshipped, like grave alchemists, the sun?

4. SAINT-LUSSON, GREEN BAY

The King of all these Frenchmen *was* the sun,
or so he liked to say, and Saint-
Lusson's vain oratory blazed with a brightness

at Green Bay outshining any local *kiktowenene's*.
But did he know to whom he spoke? Did
he know the phratries and the clans? Who was Bear

and who was Wolf or Bird, Elk or Moose or Fox?
He knew less of them than they knew
of the ones who built the mounds and made the trails

and mined the copper glowing in their lodges.
Chaskyd the ventriloquist? Wabino
eating fire? What was sleight of hand & superstition

to these soldiers of the King who sang *Vexilla Regis*
and the Jesuits who dreamed theocracy
and sought to make of these great lakes a Paraguay?

Nicholas Perrot, himself a spirit-power
said every Shaman there, assembled lines of Winnebagoes,
Potawatomies, Menomonies and Sauks before the *engagés,*

and cynical *coureurs de bois,* before the priests, before
the silken Saint-Lusson. *Vive Le Roi,* he said,
picking up a clod of earth and brandishing his sword . . .

Did Wiske smile on these transactions, throw
tobacco on the fire? and did his brother Chibyabos chant
beyond the susnset names that sounded there

like Onangizes and Onontio? *Vive Le Roi, and hail*
the highest and most mighty monarch and
most Christian King of France and of Navarre

for whom I take possession of this place Sault St. Marie
and also lakes Superior and Huron also
Manitoulin also all the countries rivers lakes and

streams contiguous adjacent thereunto both those dis-
covered and the ones we will discover
in their length & breadth & bounded only by the seas

declaring to the nations living there that they
from this time forth are vassals
of his Majesty bound by laws & customs which are his.

Then Allouez harangued them about Jesus.
Francis Parkman writes: "What remains of sovereignty
thus pompously proclaimed?

Now and then
the accents of some straggling boatman or
a half-breed vagabond—

this and nothing more."

5. MAKING OF THE RIVERS AND THE PRAIRIES

Before that rhetoric, that epigraph,
gushing of the ancient, unheard waters all along
the terminal moraine. Before the melt,

Maumee ice flow inching toward a Wabash
where no water ran, a Saginaw
into a dry Dowagiac. Before an unbound Kankakee,

glacial borders pressing ice lobes out
to flood the valley where no valley was, to spread
the drift two hundred feet and more above

Coniferous, Devonian and Trenton rock.
Before the flood, copper manitous locked up in stone
on distant islands not enisled

before the miners who would dig for them
where no mines were and build the pregnant mounds
by forest trails that were not blazed.

Before the forest trails, before the oak & ash,
path of the moraine: sand & boulders,
quartzite, clay and till . . .

Before the Potawatomies. Before the French.
Before the Studebaker &
the Bendix and the Burger Chef. . . .

            ∼

                        10,000 years ago
the Erie ice, the Saginaw,
the Michigan converged just here.

Hills and ranges fixed the contours then.
Basins formed, and runoff made
two rivers wider than the Mississippi.

Tributaries broke through lateral moraines.
The Elkhart and the Yellow rivers
drained away the last of Maumee glacier—

no waters yet could run off to Desplaines.
When they did, the two great rivers
slowed—silted up their valleys with debris

and changed their names.
Turning on itself, Dowagiac became its former
tributary, flowing to Lake Michigan.

Kankakee at flood time
emptied into the immense abandoned channel,
flowed on to St. Joseph, left

an ice gorge, then a sand bar and a bluff
here at Crum's Point.
Drainage opened to the east

all the way beyond the lakes to the St. Lawrence.
Water levels fell, channels
slowly narrowed, and the River of Miamis

took its present course. Curving to the south.
Flowing to the north.
Rising where it fell in the beginning.

So Crum's Point burst its ice-dam and
the Kankakee flowed mostly with the stronger
new and narrow river now.

Silted up to fourteen feet, the site
of a confluence sealed itself with rock
and sand and soil: made

a watershed on the continental divide.
Above, the level sand plain. And below, the marsh:
Seignelay south-west, & Illinois.

From a millennium of glacial drift, the prairies
now had formed: Portage, Palmer
Sumption ...

    Terre Coupée. . . .

   ~

       But on these waters:
Could you sail a ship?
And on this land: *Found an empire now*

    surrounded on the north and east by oak & hickory? On the
south adjoining: scattered clumps of alders, willow bushes native
to these soils. The prairie reached from portage landing two and
one half miles, three & more from the nearest eastern verge. To the
west & south, the vast expanse of grass and marsh appeared as one
great plain. Deep into the west, a stretch of rolling timber. . . .

6. THE BOAT-MAKER'S TALE

He'd sent the Griffin on back to Niagara
loaded with the furs he thought
would pay his debts. . . .
                  Colbert walked in shadows

at Versailles, the river to be named for him
named otherwise by Onangizes, called
himself, like Colbert's king, the shimmering sun.

Frontenac, Onnontio to Green Bay's Ouilamette
and all the rest of the Gigos clan,
dreamed a map of colonies and little forts

stretching from above St. Joseph on the lake
down the river of Miamis
to the marshy waters of that languid

tributary to be named one day for Seignelay
whose own necrology of ships
made him Minister among the idle admirals

in the shipyards and the ports of France.
Stretching father still . . .
Stretching well beyond that river to the one

that only Joliet and Père Marquette
among the French had ever seen & named & spoken of
saying that *no land at all no*

country would be better suited to produce
whatever fruits or wheat or corn
than that along this river that the wild cattle

never flee that one finds some 400 in a herd
that elk & deer are almost every-
where and turkeys promenade on every side. . . .

From the day a man first settled here
that man
could start to plow. . . .
                              But Cavelier, La Salle,

had sent the Griffin on back to Niagara.
He'd build a second ship
to sail down the rivers he would find. . . .

For he himself had said in Paris, sounding
just like Père Marquette, *it's all
so beautiful and fertile, free from forests*

*full of meadows brooks and rivers all
abounding there in fish & game
where flocks and herds can even be left out*

all winter long. All winter long!
And it was nearly winter now in Michillimackinak.
The King had said to him *We have received*

*with favor a petition in your name and do
permit your exploration
by these presents signed with our own hand*

but now he was in debt. Migeon, Charon—
they'd seized the beaver pelts
and even skins of skunks—Giton, Pelonquin!

Names of enemies. But there was Henri Tonty here;
there was, indeed, Count Frontenac.
Those he'd name against the plotting creditors.

The ship will fly above the crows, he'd said,
his patron governor's heraldic mast-
head besting Jesuits in a Niagaran dream of power.

He had his Récollets to do whatever of God's work
there was. Hennepin, who strapped
an altar on his back and cured the fainting

Father Gabriel with a confection of hyacinths!
and Gabriel himself; and Zénobe.
They'd sung *Te Deum* well enough upon the launching.

He'd have them sing a good deal more than that—
Exaudiat, Ludovicus Magnus!—
once they'd reach the Colbert's mouth, the sea.

The ship *had* nearly flown across the lakes.
In spite of an ungodly pilot
and in spite of god knows dreadful storms

she'd been the equal of the Erie and the Huron.
How she'd sailed out beyond Niagara!
Her canvas billowed & she fired her five small guns

to the astonishment of Iroquois along the banks.
Then a freshening northwest wind.
Down the lake and to Detroit's narrow straights

she sailed until she met a current there strong
as the bore before the lower Seine—
and twelve men leapt ashore to pull her over, through.

They marvelled at the prairies to the east & west
and stopped to hunt, and hung their
guyropes full of fowl and drying bearskins.

From wild grapes the priests prepared communion wine.
Then they were in Huron where the gale
attacked them and they brought down mainyards, tacked

with trysail, then lay long to the till.
The pilot blasphemed damnably while all the rest
cried out to Anthony of Padua

who calmed the winds and brought the ship to port
at Michillimackinak beside
the mission of St. Ignace, Père Marquette's fresh grave.

That was in the early autumn when the Ottawa
and Huron fishing fleets
were strung across the lakes from Saint Marie du Sault

to Keweenwa, from Mackinac to Onangizes' islands
in Green Bay. He'd worn his scarlet coat
with its gold lace and flown the banner of the king

while all his men fired muskets & he stepped ashore.
That was autumn, when the sun
still burned their necks & missionaries harvested.

But it was nearly winter now and he would be he said
in Illinois country when the rivers froze.
Heavy clouds blew in from Canada on northern winds.

The ship had sailed away. And so they
set forth on the lake in four canoes: fourteen men
who bore with them a forge & carpenters' &

sawyers' tools to build the Griffin's twin
beside a fort they'd also build on high ground near
the navigable lower Illinois.

They cried out to each other in the dark.
For it was dark before they were across the lake.
It stormed again as when the Griffin

rocked and shook on Huron, waves against the fragile
birchbark, rain in their red eyes.
Anvil and bellows, iron for nails and bolts,

pit-saws, arms, and merchandise for gifts
and trade when they had reached the Illinois town below
the portage weighed them down.

Gunsmith, blacksmith, joiner, mason, master-
builder Moyse Hillère—
they paddled for the farther shore with Cavelier

and three priests and the guide. Half of them
were cousins to *coureurs de bois*
and would desert. Two of them were felons.

All of them washed up together with the breaking
waves beside
the mouth of the Miamis

    and gorged on grapes and wild haws & on the carcass of a deer
that had been killed by wolves.

Here they stayed for twenty days, and built a tiny fort, and spiked
the hill they built it on. They took nine soundings of the river's
mouth, marking out the passage that a ship might take with buoys
and bearskin flags. The first brief snow blew in across the lake well
before December and ice began to form along the river's edge.
Occasionally, La Salle's Mohegan guide could find a deer to kill, or
bear, and brought them meat; but food was scarce and all of them
began to urge La Salle to press on to the portage and to Illinois or
Miami camps where they might find, in covered pits, a gleaming
hoard of winter's corn. When Tonty finally came with men who
had been sent ahead from Fort Niagara but had scattered in the
woods, the party numbered thirty-four. Four were left behind with
messages and maps for those who would arrive to reinforce them
when the Griffin sailed back past Michillimackinak and down Lake
Michigan & anchored here. If the Griffin wasn't lost. If the furs to
pay off creditors had not been stolen by the pilot and his men. If all
of them had not sailed straight to join the outlaw trader Dan Du
Lhut at Kamalastigouia up in Thunder Bay.

Nous embarquâmes, wrote Hennepin, *le troisième Decembre. Avec trente
hommes . . . Dans huit canots.* They were John Boisrondet, L'Espérance
de la Brie, La Rousselière, La Violette, Picard du Gay, Etienne

Renault, Michel Baribault, Bois d'Ardeene, Martin Chartier, Noel le Blanc, the nailer called La Forge, the Indian guide they called Oui-Oui-La-Meche, and those with names now known to all or names now known to none. They took up paddles once again, prepared to travel on, to shoulder their canoes along the portage trail if they could find it. Had it been spring, had it been high summer, the fields and woods that lined the river's channel would have blossomed for them, fruited like the prairies on the east and west of the Detroit straights when they pulled the Griffin through to Huron and the priests made wine. And when at last they reached the portage, they would have seen tall cedars, oaks and water-elms; in a ravine declining from high ground they would have seen along the curving trail splashes of the reds and blues of wild forest flowers; flocks of plovers, snipe, might have flown above the trees to land beside the standing cranes in fields of wild rice in fens the far side of the watershed across the prairie with its elk and deer and buffalo which traders would begin to call one day the *Parc aux Vaches*. But it was winter; they saw none of this. They saw the skulls and bones of animals, a bleak gray plain; they lugged their eight canoes and forge and iron and anvil up the hill and then along the portage path behind La Salle who brooded on the Griffin in the melancholy, willful, isolated silence of his mind, La Salle whose men, with five exceptions, would forsake his vision and his surrogate at Fort Crevecoeur—39 degrees and 50 minutes latitude exactly on his fine Parisian astrolabe—and daub in tar-black letters on the planking of the half-built river boat: *Nous Sommes Tous Sauvages.*

The man who followed him in many ways was like him, and read his words, and read the words and followed all the trails of others who had passed this way before he did himself, but after him who was the first to come and was the object of his search. Charlevoix he read, and La Hontan. Tonty's own account, and Hennepin's, and all of La Salle's letters both to Canada and France. Transcripts, depositions. He too knew about insatiable ambition, pride and isolation, subduing all to an inflexibility of purpose. When his chronic and mysterious illness made his head swim and his joints swell, made his eyes so sensitive to light he could not read, his nights so sleepless that he could not even dream his shattered double's thousand mile trek from the lower Illinois back to Montreal, he had his friends read *to* him, tried to comprehend their strange pronunciations of the language of the texts and maps and manuscripts *de la France Septentrionale* which he followed to the Kankakee or Seignelay and then beyond. . . .

Terres tremblantes, sur lesquelles on peut à peine marcher he read, and wrote how "soon they reached a spot where oozy saturated soil quaked beneath their tread. All around were clumps of alder-bushes . . . pools of glistening water *une espèce de mare* and in the midst a dark and lazy current, which a tall man might bestride . . . twisting like a snake among the reeds and rushes and . . . *il a faut continuellement tourner* . . . They set canoes upon this thread of water and embarked their baggage and themselves and pushed on down the sluggish streamlet looking at a little distance like men who sail on land . . . Fed by an increasing tribute of the spongy soil it widened to a river *presque aussi large que la Marne,* and they floated on their way into a voiceless, lifeless solitude of boundless marshes overgrown with reeds. . . .

At night they built their fire on ground made firm by frost
quelques mottes de terres glacées

and bivouacked among rushes . . . "

7. CONVERGENCE . . . & DISPERSION

Behind La Salle, before his blinking chronicler,
these others came. They came
to undo all designs of Tisha and his friends,

all designs conceived by Jesuit or Récollet
or empire builder in Quebec
or dreamed beneath Starved Rock among the Illinois.

These others came on urgent journeys of unmaking
and from very far away
but very fast and very quietly and no one knew.

They travelled not so much by river routes & streams
as by the trails. They came
because the French and their Algonquin allies

were establishing an iron monopoly
on furs which handsome ladies like Madame d'Outrelaise
and Madame Frontenac—les divines

they called them at Versailles—liked to drape around
their pink & chilly shoulders
when in Paris they would hear, at Arsanal,

the private recitations of Racine and Molière
or walk the Louvre along Perrault's
great colonnade, or walk le Brun's new gallery nearby.

These others walked the narrow trails
from Mohawk lodges on through busy Onondaga country
to the Senecan frontier—

These others were the Iroquois.
And when LaSalle objectively took note of 1680's comet
wondered at in Paris and the calculated

object of Sir Isaac Newton's will,
Increase Mather wrote upon the theocratic tablet of his soul:
A Portent! Well, it may have been.

Trade among the openings of oak and on the open prairie
would be anything but free.
And so they leaned into their journey, east to west,

and put a price upon it.
Over trails between the rivers flowing to the lakes
& those that flowed into the Susquehanna south—

then across the Seneca & north beyond Cayuga
to the watershed between Ontario and Erie, to Niagara.
Canadasegy, Canadaragey, Canawagus—

villages on ley lines into which their dancing feet
trod magic from the Hudson river west
and to Detroit. . . .

          ∽

                    Behind the Iroquois,
the English and the Dutch.
Behind the Dutch and English, the Americans.

Braddock, Washington. Clark & Wayne & Harrison.
The Iroquois trails and the Sauk
widened to accommodate the marching of militias—

For convergence of new peoples in procession
down new roads, dispersion's
an express condition, and diaspora's required. . . .

Pontiac's conspiracy. Tecumseh's genius
and the wild hallucinations of the Shawnee prophet
in his Prophetstown. Black Hawk for an hour.

All the rest is trade—wagons made
by Clem and Henry Studebaker in a town Coquillard
founded for the Astors.

Oh, and Cooper's wooden Indians.
Standing near the banks of local rivers in his book
of 1848, they decorate a prairie

modelled now on European parks mown by gardeners
who themselves become like trees
on the green & flowering stage which they prepare

a decade after the removal of the Potawatomis.
They stand there like Pokagon, last
okama of the lakes whose little band did not accept

the Treaty of Chicago engineered by Billy Caldwell
but remained in his protection
and in his most pious Christian prayers, and even

in his fiction ghosted by a local lawyer's wife
whose husband pressed his claims
in every court. Cooper's stagecoach, meanwhile,

clatters past the Walker Tavern on the old Sauk trail
that's become the route of Western's
bright red buckboards & their Concord Coaches from Detroit.

The aging author whose new book will be dismissed
for tedious didacticism & a meager plot
engages Mrs. Martineau from London in a civil conversation

interrupted by her not infrequent jottings in a diary
about how wisely planned
and prettily she finds this road from Niles

which the Iroquois took to slaughter Illinois women
at Starved Rock and which, from
Ypsilanti down to Edwardsburg and then beyond

80,000 western emigrants began to stream by 1838 or 39.
We cross St. Joseph's River,
Mrs. Martineau observes, *upon a ferry towed by ropes.*

And as the clever horses pull us up the bank
we find ourselves in Indiana territory. She glances up
at Cooper who, in turn, acknowledges her smile.

The stagecoach travels on. Arriving from Fort Wayne,
and heading north & west along
what still they call the Dragoon Trail, the U.S. mail . . .

while ahead of it, turning just in front of Cooper's
coach on Michigan, honking Studebakers
and the children marching smartly off in little groups

before the dignitaries—councilman & mayor
& some Elks & Shriners dressed to look like Potawatami
and Illinois elders—

and everybody smiling at the camera
as if this were
some kind of local pageant

~

    & they gathered near the portage trail
to commemorate La Salle in a depression.
Hoover, says the Mayor, will employ honest citizens

to build a great historic monument. A corner
stone is laid. Massed bands of high school students play,
choirs singing in the cold . . . *Semper Fidelis.*

December 5, 1679. *Queleques mottes de terres glacés.*
Eight years later and
La Salle was murdered by conspirators in Texas.

A bell tower rises, in a man's imagination,
some two hundred feet. (The monument was never built.)
On the river, down below the pageant,

in a man's imagination or before him on his page
Now and then
the accents of a straggling boatman

or a half-breed vagabond
this &
nothing more . . .

Part II

Survivors

I

A letter arrives in answer
To mine—but six years late . . .
"John," it says,
                    "Dear John . . . " and
"I remember absolutely nothing.
What you say is probably
All true; for me those
Years are blank. I believe
You when you say you knew
Me then, that we were friends,
And yet I don't remember you
At all, or all those others
Who had names, or anyone. You see,

The fittest don't survive—
It's the survivors."

II

Like old women, burying their
Husbands, burying their sons, lasting
It out for years without their breasts
Or wombs, with ancient eyes,
Arthritic hands, and memories like
Gorgeous ships they launch
Despairingly to bring back all
Their dead, and which, as if constructed
By some clumsy sonneteer, betray them
Instantly and sink without a trace.

III

Or women not so old—
                    but always
Women, not the men who knock
Their brains and bodies against
Fatal obstacles & spit their blood
On pillows & their hearts on sleeves
At forty-five to die of being fit.

I've known a woman keep her watch
Beside a bed of botched ambition
Where her man lay down & took
Five years to die . . .

And though I drove one January night
Through freezing rain into Ohio—
And though I hurried,
Seeking the words of the dying—
All I found was a turning circle of women,
All I heard was the lamentation of survivors.

Edward

Edward, Edward, how we fear the sick!
I think I can almost remember you
whose name I'm called, John Edward.
Your illness was a terror
for us all. We, your nephews, marvelled
in our fear. We didn't know
exactly what the sick know, but we
knew they know—O things forbidden to the fit.
You were a kind of Shaman for us then.

We watched you jerk from chair
to cane, we watched you jam your gears, repeat,
walk backwards through the door,
then freeze and point, all man of ice,
at something moving after it had moved,
and then unfreeze, unlock,
and then repeat: *I do it then, I do it then.*

You gave us candies made of malted milk
and the family left you dying
in your corner chair. You had the post-war
sleeping-sickness, and you mostly slept:
through our lives, through your own.
There seemed no pity for you in that house.
For me, it was a magic time. I loved
my cousin then the way a boy of eight can
love a boy of ten. What could any of us do
for you? We took your candy and we fled.

Everybody fled: to their lunches or their jobs,
to their games or their affairs.
The other, boozy uncle said: *He was an ass-man once.*
For days I wondered what he meant.
Edward, did you curse us all the way you
might have, Shaman-like and darkly, silently:
So go off to your God-damned job and leave me here.
Your lunch. Your girl. Kid, go ride your bike
into a fucking truck. Who knows what you thought.
The children fled with the adults.

But when your brother in his final illness wept,
and when I had no pity, when I couldn't
stand to hear him say like any eight-year-old:
You made me cry, and when he said just audibly
enough for me to hear: *Go back to your*
God-damned books, then, Edward, I thought
I could remember you almost
and me a book-man, not an ass-man, now.
Edward, Edward, how we fear the sick!
Such counsels O
they give us of mortality.

U.S.I.S. Lecturer

—*Amsterdam, Kalverstraat, March*

What I hear at first is *Heren* and then *Heroine.*
Then the sudden toothy Dutchman
Ages dreadfully and vaguely threatens
Something, turns American,
And says with perfect clarity: "Heroin,

Like *smack."* We stare each other down.
Eyes gone, muscles gone, he is teeth & yellow paper.
Still, I sense he is about my age.
I brush on past him, mind all wheeling
Backwards out of gear

To 1961 when I was here before and just eighteen.
What I dreamed into the streets of Amsterdam
Was Love: pure, high, unyielding,
Disdainful, and serene.
An appallingly beautiful bawd said she'd

Take my friend and me together. He
Went in alone, and for a moment I could see
Them swimming in the gaudy lights
Behind her fishbowl window. Someone opened up
A paper and I read: *Hemingway Zelfmoord.*

A decade and a half. I'm here to lecture twice
On a man who was my teacher once
Who, that very afternoon, in hot America,
Sat down aching and wrote out:
"My mother has your shotgun." And:

"It's so I broke down here."
In the middle of his poem, he meant.
I heard myself quote Woody Allen to a group
Of students yesterday in Leiden when
They asked me what I thought they could believe in.

Sex and death, I said.
Part of me's gone rotten as my junkie-brother's eyes.
Respectful and respectable, I took
A check from my ambassador
And quoted Woody Allen's quip to get a laugh.

I forgot to say: *"It was as he wrote his poem,*
You understand. His father
Had self-murdered too." Somewhere there,
In 1961 or so, was Love.
I'll think about the man who wrote the poem.

If Not a Technical Song American:
Statement, Harangue, and Narrative

I STATEMENT

Just last night I read your poems to the President.
You don't believe me, but I really did.
He broke down completely and
Wept all over his desk.
Now that I've done my work, you can relax.
Everything's going to be o.k.

And I read your poems to a joint session of Congress.
I read your poems to the FBI and the CIA.
Now that I've done my work, you can relax.
Everything's going to be o.k.

II HARANGUE

Your tired evasions, euphemism-lies.
Civilized man and his word-hoard.
Will you be relinquant
Or relinquished.

Name and Title. Religion and Rank.
Put a check in the column.
Put a check in the bank.

If you'd be only a little bit clever.
If you'd be occasionally.
If you'd be forever.

If you'd be my government.
If you'd be my gal.
If you'd be my treason and my tongue.

If anything articulate remains,
Identify the numbers by the names.

III NARRATIVE

Cachectic, cachectic.
Heart rate grossly irregular.
Jugular venous distention.
Systolic expansile pulse.

Right ventricular lift.
Left ventricular tap.
Murmur along the sternal borders.
Pulmonary edema.

All piezometers installed
In the boreholes.
Static and dynamic
Cone penetration made.

Infra-red results
Allow mathematical models.
I hope I was never
Complacent: Seismology.

BUT IF I WAS IN LOVE WITH YOU?
I was in love with you, I think.
I think I didn't have the heart.

No, I never even thought to move the earth.

For John, After His Visit: Suffolk, Fall

Soldati's band shook Patty Fenelon's house
    last Spring so badly that the
Bookcase toppled down and spilled the cheap
    red wine on three authentic South
Bend, Indiana drunks. . . .
                   For you, who love
    the elegiac and, if you believed
The arts you practice had in fact a chance
    of life at all, would prophesy
A new Romantic muse for all of us, how
    can I speak generously enough
About the life we've shared—the rich neurotic
    squalor of the midwest's Catholic
Mecca (. . . you a convert, me a Roman guest—
    cloistered there together preaching
Culture to the grandsons of Italian immigrants,
    the sons of Irishmen and Poles)?

You must, you always told me,
    have intensity. Half your students
Always thought you mad. Like Gordon
    Liddy on a job you'd go
To them bewigged and bearded bearing with
    you some incongruous foreign
Object—a Henry James harpoon or a Melvillian
    top hat—while through the hidden
Speakers blared your tape of Colin Davis and
    the BBC crooning Elgar on the
Last night of the Proms. Light in darkness, John!
    And all your manic gestures were serene.

Yeats to Lady Gregory, Nineteen Hundred & Four:
    "I did not succeed at Notre Dame."
He began to think his notions seemed "the thunder
    of a battle in some other star"; the thought
Confused him and he lectured badly; later he
    told tales with the "merry priests."
So you were not the first to feel estranged! And
    oh the thunder of your battle in that
Other star, its foolishness and grace. Beyond that
    fiddle, though, intensity was real
Enough for both of us.

How was I to know, returning from the dusty
    attic room where I had gone, where
I had often gone from midnight until three, and
    seeing you stare vacantly across
Your desk and through your lighted study
    window at the February snow that
You should truly be in love with my young
    friend, with that same lonely girl?

Was that the week you thought your son was ill?
    When you waited frightened while the
Severed head of Johnny's siamese cat melted grinning
    in its package of dry ice padlocked in
The Greyhound baggage room in Indianapolis? The
    tests were negative, the bites
And scratches healed. . . .
                    Hiking on a treadmill
        at the clinic, I tested badly on a

Winter afternoon myself. I traded polysyllables
        with cardiologists who hooked me to their
Apparatus, checked my pressures, watched my blips
        on television screens, and asked me all
The secrets of my heart....

Once we hiked together on the muddy banks of the
        St. Joseph, then across a farm. Your
Children ran ahead. They led you, while you
        talked in words they could not hear,
Haranguing me about the words you sometimes spoke
        when you would only speak, to credit
For a moment, because they looked at all around
        them, tree and bush and flower, because
They did not name and did not need to name, the
        eluctable modality of all you saw.

What more homely elegiacs, John, than this:
        reading backwards in a diary from
May—May to January, January twenty-fifth . . . and
        all my pulses skip. My father's gestures
Of exhausted resignation cease; he drops his cup
        of Ovaltine and stares into my
Mother's eyes amazed.... No dream, even, did he
        send me in my mourning time, no news
At all.... As a child I saw irregularities signaled
        in the pulsings of distended veins
Running up his temples and across his wrists:
        more affaires de cœur....
                                You made
Your trip among the dead ten years ago
        but found a Christian God along

The way in Barcelona. Did I take for politics
    your strange Falangist quips
The day we met?

December last, a month before my father's death,
    a quiet Christmas eve with sentimental
And nostalgic talk, some carolling. . . . Suddenly
    the blood. Stalking through a dark
And quiet house with automatic rifle and grenades
    you'd kick a bedroom door to bits and
Blast the sleeping couple in their bed, sprinkling
    holy water everywhere—your own obsessive
Dream. "I must have savagery," a wealthy British
    poet told me, leaving for the States.
I've gone the other way. My next door neighbor
    pounded at my door on Christmas eve; his
Bleeding wounds were real. What was all of England
    to a single one of his desires? When
I needed help you harbored me.

I wonder if our quarrel touches writing desks,
    like Mandelstam's with Pasternak. The
Harrowed man required none, the other poet did.
    Behind each artifact of any worth,
Cocteau insists, there is a house, a lamp, a fire,
    a plate of soup, a rack of pipes,
And wine. The bourgeoisie as bedrock. Mandelstam
    would crouch in corners listening to
The burning in his brain. If you're a Russian
    Jew because I am a wanton I am Catholic.

So what's the Devil's wage? Your riddling military
        metaphors unwind from Clausewitz and you
Will not say; your Faust, de Sade in near quotations
        will not do. In London monographs on
Mahler are delivered in the morning post intended
        for the eyes of diplomats on holiday in
Devon—the still & deadly music of the IRA. One
        by one these books explode . . . In the hands
Of an unlucky clerk, the lap of an astonished secretary
        dreaming of her lover.

Stranger, then, and brother! John, these last three
        nights I've listened for you here,
Listened for you here where off the North Sea
        early Autumn winds bring down the
Twigs and bang the shutters of this house
        you came to bringing with you
Secrets and your difficult soul. In disintegrating
        space we are an architecture of sounds.
And you are not returning.

Once for English Music

I

This, this is marvelous,
    this is simply too good—
I am their song, Jeremiah!
    Elgar on The Folk.

And I have worked for forty years
    and Providence denies
Me hearing of my work. So I submit:
    God is against it,

Against art. And I have worked
    for forty years and
Providence denies. And Strauss (R.),
    1905: I drink

To the welfare of the first
    English progressive.
And Gerontius: pray for me, my friends,
    who have no strength to pray.

II

And who would not put out—with his mother
Or his Queen—the night light,

Toothbrush, bathrobe and condom,
Run the bath, switch on the stereo,

Plug in the fire, and wait for time
To reverse, wait for a Prince to rise

From the dead & conduct his affairs?
Neither you nor I, neither mine nor yours.

III

There in the James Gunn portrait,
There, almost, in the Beecham life—

Delius who wasn't really English,
Delius who got around:

Dying, did he summon in his cripple's dream
A syphilitic and promiscuous librettist

(In a summer garden, or on hearing the
First cuckoo in Spring)?

He would compose.
He would have his way with words.

IV

During the performance
        of an overture, said Shaw,
By one of the minor Bachs,
        I was annoyed
By what I took to be the jingling
        of a bell-wire somewhere.
But it was Dr. Parry. Playing the
        cembalo part . . . on a
Decrepit harpsichord.

V

Fluctuating sevenths,
        fluctuating thirds.
I'll play it on my flute
        the way it sounds.

In Surrey, in Sussex,
        airs against the harmon-
Izing organist from
        Worthing. . . .

For Why Do The Roses?
        Because we sing enchanted.
Because we chant
        And sing.

Three Around a Revolution

I A Gift

He is the Tribune of The People,
He is Babeuf. The others speculate,

But he is Babeuf. The others
Speculate and steal. Gracchus

Out of Plutarch, he takes
The crudely fashioned knife

Made by his son from a candlestick
For his (the father's) suicide.

He hones it on his eloquent tongue.
He says, smiling enigmatically:

Here, it is yours. Do what you can.

II Alternatives

One announces in papers:
Seeking the patronage of the rich

To further my work. For a decade
It will always be noon.

Nobody's wealth intervenes
Between freedom and time.

One in despair discharges a gun:
Nevertheless, he goes on writing

Noblesse oblige with seven balls
Of shot in his brain.

Making accurate measurements,
Another says: Here we may build,

Here we may bathe, here we may breathe.

III A LETTER

There must be horses, there must be women,
There must be lawsuits. There must, moreover

And eventually, be justice. There must be words.
I write down words. Are we lost in our names?

Yesterday I spoke for hours and nobody stirred.
Rapt. They cheered. I am a hero.

I said words like *action, money, love, rights*
And was moved to elegance, alliteration,

Saying, apropos of what I did not know,
Palfrey, palindrome, pailing, palinode, palisade.

Alexander Kerensky at Stanford

He rose one Winter from his books
To sit among the young, unrecognized.

It was 1963. It was 1917.
He sipped his coffee & was quite anonymous.

Students sat around him at their union
Talking politics: Berkeley, Mississippi.

A sun-tanned blonde whose wealthy father
Gave her all his looks and half his money

Whispered to her sun-tanned lover:
"Where *is* Viet Nam?"

He thought no thought of theirs.
In his carrel at the Hoover Institute

He had the urns of all his ancient enemies.
Their dust was splattered on his purple tie.

Double Sonnet on the Absence of Text:
"Symphony Matis der Maler,"
Berlin, 1934:—Metamorphoses

I

The eschatology of Jews and Christian heretics:
Unearthly metal glows. *Schafft er night mehr—*
He lies among his tools.
Geh hin und bilde. Geh hin und bilde
Polyptich as polyphony. Medieval modes,
Matis: Gothardt, Neithardt. Grunewald
To historians, *der Maler.*
Father of no child though, Regina; father
Of is altarpiece at Isenheim, father
Of his torments, his tormentors,
Dying in obscurity at Halle building mills.
Geh hin und bilde. For Albricht, Luther
Or for Muntzer? *Geh hin und bilde.*
The pointing finger of an evangelic hand
Outlasts apocalypse.

II

The libretto: that's the crux, the words.
Because of that the senile Strauss would
Play *Gebrauchsmusik* for Goebbels who, while
Furtwängler's applauded by the partisans
Of Brecht or Grosz or Benn, sits
On hams beside the corpse of Wagner.
Oh that Hindemith should feel the pull
Of Matis: What's the distance, then, from
Buchenwald to Yale? *Ist, dass du
Schaffst und bildest, genug?*
Abandoned, all the words: for what
They cannot settle will be left alone.
Leaving us just where, Professor?
Contemplating cosmogonic harmonies with Kepler.
In oblivion with courage and acoustics.

Turns: Toward a Provisional Aesthetic
and a Discipline

I

The scolemayster levande was the toun
and sary of hit semed everuch one.
The smal quyt cart that covert was and hors . . .
to ferien his godes. To ferien his godes
quere he was boun.

The onelych thyng of combraunce (combraunce)
was the symphonye
(saf a pakke of bokes)
that he hade boghte the yere
quen he bithoght
that he wolde lerne to play.

But the zele woned (zele woned).
He neuer couthe ani scylle.

II

And so the equivalent
        (the satisfactory text.
squ'elles sont belles
        sont pas fidèles. rough
west-midland, hwilum andgit
of andgiete: the rest is not
        a word for word defense. . . .

III

And make him known to 14th-century men
Even when everything favors the living?
Even if we could reverse that here
I know you've read and traveled too.

So Destination or Destiny: *Quere He was Boun!*
And yet to introduce the antecedent place.
Restrictive clause; sense of the referent noun.
A tilted cart is a cart with an awning.

> Langland has it "keured"
> John of Mandeville "coured"
> Wycliffe "keuered"

> But "covert" in Arimathaea

Personal luggage: not the same as merchandise.
Cursor Mundi's "gudes;" Purity's "godes"

This is personal luggage / destination / travel

> Harp and pipe and symphonye

> (saf a pakke of bokes)

IV

Where dwelle ye if it tell to be?

> at the edge
> of the toun?

at the edge
of the toun?

Levande was.
He Levande Was The Toun.

Reason the nature of place
Reason he can praise
Reason what the good-doing doctor said

Rx.:cart   (that covert was & hors)

Dull ache in the hip is probably gout.
Painful nodes of calcium—(neck & in the ears).
Palpitations, flutters. Stones in the gland.

food to avoid?   drink

(put him in the cart)

Rx.:bibliography
Rx.:map

V

The metaphysicality of Hermetic thought—
Let him think o' that! (Problem is he
Still enjoys cunt . . .)

. . . instrument was ay thereafter
Al his own combraunce . . .

Sary of hit semed everuch one.

Torn between disgust & hope
He simply never couthe ...

antiquorum aegyptiorum
oh, ... imitatus ...

VI

All day long it rains. He travels
All day long. Wiping water from
His eyes: and twenty miles? and
Twenty miles? Fydlers nod & smile.

Cycles pass him. Cars pass him.
Buses full of tourists ...
Dauncers & Minstrels, Drunkards
And Theeves. Whooremaisters,
Tossepottes; Maskers, Fencers
And Rogues; Cutpurses, Blasphemers
Counterfaite Egyptions ...

Greek, Arabic, Medieval Latin,
Mis-translated, misconceived.
More than just for his disport

        who loveth daliaunce

who falleth   (o who falleth)

far behinde ...

VII

That supernatural science,
That rare art should seem ...

    here among
    a randy
    black-billed

    ilk

Les traductions sont comme les femmes. And time to get off of her
toes. Idiomatic: toes. Lorsqu'elles sont belles. I should apologize,
then: to apologize. The schoolmaster was leaving the village, and
everybody seemed sorry. Simple as that. The miller lent him the
cart and horse to carry his goods. Simple as that. And no particular
trouble with the words. Scolemayster: 1225 in the *Life of St
Katherine*. But you change the spelling, see, to conform with the
dialect. Levande was: *The Destruction of Troy*, "all the Troiens lefton."
But use the participial construction. Sary of hit: see the *Lay Folks
Mass Book*. The city of his destination. Twenty miles off. Quite
sufficient size for his effects. The only cumbersome article (save the
pack of books) was: count on the medieval mind to be sympathetic.
Though I come after hym with hawebake/I speke in prose and lat
hym rymes make. My general principles I take from the King (and
his Queen). Tha boc wendan on Englisc. Hwilum word be word.
Hwilum andgit of andgiete. Swa swa ic hie geliornode. It would be
idle and boring to rehearse. Here what is available. Let me simply
indicate the manner. Take sulphur from Sol for the fire and with
it roast Luna. From which will the word issue forth. . . . *If* the given
appeared in a verifiable text. . . . *If* the given was truly equivalent.

The usual procedures are the following: (1) To ignore altogether: "make no effort to explain the fundamentals." (2) To drop apologetic footnotes: "I'm sorry, but I simply cannot understand this esoteric sort of thing." (3) To make suggestive remarks while hurrying on to something else: "*If* the given appeared in a verifiable text. *If* the given was truly equivalent." But the schoolmaster was leaving the village, and everybody seemed sorry. *Jude the Obscure*, paragraph one, a neat linguistic exercise. Written by Thomas Hardy in 1895. And such a revelation makes the art available to the vulgar. Who will abuse and discredit? *Keeper of secret wisdom, agent of revelation, vision and desire:* THIS IS THE QUESTION WE MUST ALWAYS RAISE.

Now some of the obscure, like some of the lucid, do not become proletarianized. Unlike the majority of their kind, they are not cast down from the ruling class to produce a commodity which both enslaves them and enslaves the exploited labourers with whom they are objectively allied. Perhaps they hold teaching jobs in public schools or universities; perhaps they have an inherited income. In any case, some maintain their Hermetic privilege. They are not obliged to live by their art or to produce for the open market. Such unproletarianized obscure are revolted by the demands of a commercialized market, by the vulgarity of the mass-produced commodity suppled to meet it. And revulsion ultimately tells (1) on their sex life (2) on their health.

While a relationship of cause and effect is established between obscure and lucid organizations emerging from the division of labour and the consequent dialectical evolution of social reality, such becomes, we know, increasingly separated from the actual productive function of society, from sleep. This gives us pause. "The point is that the notion of invariancy inherent by definition to the concept of the series, if applied to all parameters, leads to a uniformity of configurations that eliminates the last traces of unpredictability, of surprise." This gives us pause.

And so the system and its adherents are the villains; license, conspiracy, and nihilism are the virtues of the heroes: *or*: The system itself becomes a context for heroics; license, conspiracy, and nihilism become the crimes of the villains; acceptance of convention and austere self-discipline become the virtues of the heroes. The schoolmaster is forever an intermediary: the shape of his life is determined by the nature of society: the nature of his art seeks to determine the shape of society by administering to its nature. And intermediacy ultimately tells (1) on his sex life (2) on his health.

But make him known to 14th-century men even when everything favors the living. Reason the nature of place. Reason he can praise. Reason that he travels in a cart. With Cursor Mundi's "gudes"; with Purity's "godes." With Joseph of Arimathaea, turns: to elliptically gloss.

Double Derivation, Association, and Cliché:
from *The Great Tournament Roll*
of Westminster

I

The heralds wear their tabards correctly.
Each, in his left hand, carries a wand.
Before and after the Master of Armour
Enter his men: three of them carry the staves.
The mace bearer wears a yellow robe.
In right & goodly devysis of apparyl
The gentlemen ride.
The double-curving trumpets shine.

Who breaks a spear is worth the prize.

II

Or makes a forest in the halls of Blackfriars
at Ludgate whych is garneychyd wyth trees & bowes,
wyth bestes and byrds; wyth a mayden
syttyng by a kastell makyng garlonds there;
wyth men in woodwoos dress,
wyth men of armes. . . .
                    Or Richard Gibson
                         busy
with artificers and labour, portages and ships:
busy with his sums and his accounts:
for what is wrought by carpenters & joyners,
karrovers & smiths . . .
(Who breaks a spear is worth the prize)
Who breaks a schylld on shields
a saylle on sails
a sclev upon his lady's sleeves;
who can do skilfully the spleter werke,

whose spyndylles turn

Power out of parsimony, feasting
Out of famine, revels out of revelation:—
Out of slaughter, ceremony.
When the mist lifts over Bosworth.
When the mist settles on Flodden.

Who breaks a spear is worth the prize.

  III

The double-curving trumpets shine:
  & cloth of gold.
The challengers pass . . .

Well, & the advice of Harry Seven:—
(or the Empress Wu, depending
where you are):
We'll put on elegance later.
We'll put off art.
No life of Harry the Seven
  there in the works of the Bard . . .
(No Li Po on Wu)
An uninteresting man? Parsimonious.

Wolsey travels in style . . .
     & on the Field of Cloth of Gold
  & in the halls at Ludgate
a little style. . . .
Something neo-Burgundian
(Holy, Roman & bankrupt) illuminating

Burgkmairs in *Der Weisskunig & Freydal*.
Rival Maximilian's mummeries, his
dances and his masques, his
armouries & armourers the mark.
Hammermen to King, his prize; King
to hammermen: guard, for love of progeny,
the private parts!
                    (My prick's bigger
than *your* prick, or Maxi's prick,
or James')

          IV

          & like the Burgkmairs
these illuminations:—
where, o years ago, say twenty-two or
say about five hundred,
cousins in the summertime would
ritualize their rivalries
in sumptuous tableaux.
Someone holds a camera. Snap.
In proper costume, Homo Ludens wears
Imagination on his sleeve.

But chronicle & contour fashion
out of Flodden nothing but the truth.
The deaths, in order & with dignity,
of every child: I remember that.

Who breaks a spear is worth the prize.

V

Who breaks a schylld on shields
    a saylle on sails
a sclev upon his lady's sleeves ...
And in the north, & for the nearer rival.
Who meteth Coronall to Coronall, who beareth
a man down:—down the distance to Westminster,
down the distance in time.

For the pupil of Erasmus,
for the rival of the Eighth,
a suitcase dated Flodden full of relics.
Shipped Air France, they're scattered
at the battle of the Somme.
It intervened, the news:
it intervenes

As, at the Bankside, Henry makes
a masque at Wolsey's house and, certain
cannons being fired, the paper
wherewith one of them is stopped
does light the thatch, where being
thought at first but idle smoke,
it kindles inwardly consuming
in the end
the house
the Globe

        The first & happiest hearers of the town
        among them, one Sir Henry Wotton

Largely Fletcher's work

VI

O, largely spleter werke
that certain letters could be sent
unto the high & noble excellent Princess
the Queen of England from her dear & best beloved
Cousin Noble Cueur Loyall with knowledge of
the good and gracious fortune of the birth
of a young prince:
                    & to accomplish certain
feats of arms the king (signed Henry R)
does send four knights . . .

        & sends to work his servant Richard Gibson
on the Revels and Accounts
& sends the children in the summertime to play
& sends the rival Scott a fatal surrogate
from Bosworth, makes an end
to *his* magnificence.

Slaughter out of ceremony, famine
out of feasting, out of power
parsimony, out of revels
revelation . . .

            As an axe in the spine can reveal,
        as an arrow in the eye.

Who breaks a spear is worth the prize.

VII

And what is wrought by carpenters & joyners,
by karrovers & smiths, is worth the prize;
and what is wrought by labour.
For those who play. Of alldyr pooles & paper,
whyght leed and gleew, yern hoopes of sundry
sortes; kord & roopes & naylles:—
All garneychyd at Ludgate. With
trees & bows. All garneychyd with
cloth of Gold.

The challengers pass

And deck themselves outrageously
in capes & plumes and armour ...
And out to play: making in the summertime
a world against all odds, and with
its Winter dangers.

In a garden, old men play at chess.
In the Summer. In the Winter, still.

Who will decorate the golden tree,
Employ properly the captive giant
And the dwarf? Who will plead
His rights despite decrepitude ... ?

I reach for words as in a photograph
I reach for costumes in a trunk:

An ancient trunk (an ancient book)

a saylle, a schylld, a sclev

a yellow robe, a wand—

    pipes & harpes & rebecs,
    lutes & viols for a masque.

Where double-curving trumpets shine
The challengers pass.

Who breaks a spear is worth the prize.

Clarifications for Robert Jacoby
("Double Derivation . . . ", Part IV, ll. 1–10; Part VII, ll. 1–15, 22–28)

A moment ago, Robert, I thought I was watching
    a wren, the one which nests
By my window here, fly, dipping & rising,
    across this field in Suffolk
So like the one we used to play in, in Ohio,
    when we were boys. But it was
Really something that you, Dr Jacoby, would
    be able to explain by pointing out
To me in some expensive, ophthalmological text
    the proper Latin words.

It was no wren (still less the mythological bird
    I might have tried to make it)—
But just defective vision: one of those spots
    or floating motes before the eyes
That send one finally to a specialist. Not
    a feathered or a golden bird,
Nothing coming toward me in the early evening
    mist, just a flaw, as they say,
In the eye of the beholder.

Like? in a way?
    the flaw in the printer's eye
(the typesetter's, the proof-
    reader's) that produced and then
Let stand that famous line
    in Thomas Nashe's poem about the plague,
"Brightness falls from the air,"
    when what he wrote was, thinking
Of old age and death, "Brightness
    falls from the *hair*."

I wonder if you remember all those games
    we used to play: the costumes,
All the sticks & staves, the whole complicated
    paraphernalia accumulated to suggest
Authentic weaponry and precise historical dates,
    not to mention exact geographical places,
All through August and September—the months you
    visited. You wanted then, you said,
To be an actor, and your father—a very practical
    lawyer—said he found that funny, though
I think we both intuited
    that he was secretly alarmed.

With little cause. You were destined—how obvious
    it should have been!—to be professional,
Respectable, and eminent. Still, you put in time
    and played your child's part
With skill and grace.

There is a photograph of us taken, I believe,
    in 1950. Your plumed hat (a little
Tight) sits sprightly on your head, your cape
    (cut from someone's bathrobe) hangs
Absurdly down your back, and in your hand you
    brandish the sword of the patriarch
Himself, grandfather M., Commander in Chief
    Of the United Spanish War Vets.
                        My
Plumed hat is slightly better fitting, if less
    elegant, my sword a fencing foil with
A rubber tip, my cape the prize: something from
    the almost legitimate theatre, from
My father's role in a Masonic play where he spoke,

once each year before initiations
On some secret, adult stage, lines he practiced
    in the kitchen all the week before:
Let the jewelled box of records be opened
    and the plans for the wall by the
South west gate be examined!

The photographer, it seems, has irritated us.
    We scowl. The poses are not natural.
Someone has said Simon says stand here, look
    there, dress right, flank left;
Someone, for the record, intervenes. Or has
    James arrived? Our cousin from the
East side of Columbus who, with bicycles
    and paper routes and baseballs
Wanted you in time as badly then as I could
    want you out of it. A miniature
Adult, he looked askance at our elaborate
    rituals. He laughed outright,
Derisively. No mere chronicler, he was reality
    itself. I hated him.

Of whom I would remind myself when asking you:
    do you remember? a world of imagination,
Lovely and legitimate, uncovering, summer after
    summer, a place that we no longer go,
A field we do not enter now, a world one tries
    to speak of, one way or another,
In a poem. Robert! Had the jewelled box
    of records been opened and the plans
For the wall by the south west gate been examined,
    news: that he, not you and I, made
Without our knowledge, without our wigs and

epaulets, with bricks he had a right
To throw, binding rules for our splendid games.

How remote it all must seem to you who joined
        him with such dispatch. One day, I
Suppose, I'll come to you in California saying
        to you frankly: cure me if you can.
Or to some other practicing your arts. Until then,
        what is there to talk about except
This book of photographs? And what they might
        have made of us, all those aunts,
Clucking at our heels, waddling onto Bosworth field
        or Flodden with their cameras. And why
They should have come, so ordinary and so mortal,
        to bring back images like this one
Turning yellow in a yellow book. Brightness fell
        from the hair

Of whom I would be worthy now, of whom I think
        about again as just outside my window
A child plays with a stick. And jumps on both feet
        imitating, since she sees it in the field
(With a stick in its beak), a wren. She enters
        the poem as she enters the field. I will
Not see her again. She goes to her world of stick
        and field and wren; I go to my world
Of poem. She does not know it, and yet she is here:
        here in the poem as surely as there
In the field, in the dull evening light, in the world
        of her imagining, where, as the mist descends,
She is a wren.

As I write that down she is leaving the field.
        She goes to her house where her
Father and mother argue incessantly, where
        her brother is sick. In the house
They are phoning a doctor. In the poem—
        because I say so,
                        because I say once more
That she enters the world of her imagining
        where, as the mist descends,
She is a wren—
        She remains in the field.

Poem for Cynouai

I

With urgency and passion you argue for the lot—
every one of thirty watercolors
ranged in retrospective
which I thought to choose among.
Circumspect, I sought
negotiations. You squint your lazy eye
and wave your arm in arcs
around our geocentric circle and insist:
"We'll take them all!"

II

I am easily persuaded.
How luminous their rendering of a world
we both believe in
and can sometimes share:—
where names are properties of things
they name, where stones
are animate and wilful, trees
cry out in storms, and compulsive
repetition of the efficacious formulae
will get us each his way.

When they patched your overcompensating eye
your work began. Your starboard
hemisphere was starved for colors
and for shapes.
Suddenly a punning and holistic
gnostic, you painted
everything in sight:
your left eye flashed at cats & camels

in the clouds, while one by one
you drew them with a shrewd right hand
into a white corral.
At school they said your "problem"
was "perceptual."

III

What did you perceive,
and what did I?
I found that scattering of words
in notes. I wrote it down
two years ago and now you do not paint.
I no longer wrote. It's out
of date, we've changed.
I was going to quote Piaget
and go on to talk about perception.
Instead I went to work
and earned some money, girl.
I was going to call
you *child*.

Two years, then. We'll keep it honest
as I wander back with you
to Shelford. Bob & Earlene live in Shelford
now, Leif and Luke and Kristin.
Bob has poems in which
he whispers *child, child.*
"We'll take them all," you said,
and I said
I am easily persuaded.
We took just one.

IV

But it is altogether marvelous.
I've kept it here while
you've gone riding with your friends.
Your passion now is horses.
It feels as if you've been away two years—
two years.
Stout-hearted Moshe,
peering one-eyed through your
horse's ears, this bright Ikon that
you've left me makes me
think of William Blake's *Glad Day.*
One sad poet wrote: My
daughter's heavier. And another:
O may she be beautiful, but
not *that* beautiful. I have a friend
who's visited Ms. Yeats—
She's bald with warts! O daughters
and their bright glad days
growing beautiful or heavier or bald.
O foolish leers and Lears.

We played. And we play now, but
not so much. Our problem
was perceptual. I think we were
perhaps too Japanese:
I have it on authority
that formal speech retains
the spirit of *bushido* in Japan.
In the *asobase-Kotaba*
we don't say: "I'm here in Shelford"
or "You're riding"

but: "I pretend to be in Shelford"
or "You play at
going riding." Nor does one say:
"I hear your father's dead,"
but this instead:
"I understand your father
has played dying."

V

When my father finished playing dying
I began.
You gave me pictures
which I held against a wound.
I wrote: "How luminous their rendering
of a world we both believe in"
and then I think you stopped believing. . . .

For money, with a friend,
I helped to translate Lars Norén
who far away
in dark, cold Sweden wrote:

Today I see that my daughter
is higher, greater
than I, and completed . . . Her
hard Kaiser head encircles me & carries
me and helps me. Silently
we speak in each other—Then
she paves the dead ones.
She comes towards me in her Kaiser skirt.

How I stumbled after you with memories & books.
How far ahead you rode. How very
quickly all the books
were closed. How frightening the horses are

As you approach me on The Black Duke of Norfolk.
The Duke's Funeral Helm is low on your eyes
(I stole it for you from a golden nail
in Framlingham church).
Your Ming Dynasty jodhpurs cling to your legs,
cling to your horse's sides
(I sent for them express to Rajasthan).
Your Dalai Lama coat is zipped up tight
(I zipped it up myself).
Your green Tzarina vest divests me.
Your beady Pony Club badge is a third eye
pinned to your cheating heart.
On a velvet photograph of Princess Anne
you are riding in circles of dust.
One eye is patched, old pirate,
and the other eye is glazed.
Only the third one, the Pony Club badge,
can see me, and it stares,
fiery and triumphant.
You are riding in circles of dust.
You are riding into the eye of the Pony Club badge.

First they patched your eye
and then I saw.
My problem was perceptual.

Lars Norén concludes:
She hungers after herself. . . .

VI

What I had wanted to say was: *red, ocher,*
orange, blue, green, violet.
What I had wanted to say was: *grass, sky,*
sun, moon, child, forest, sea.
I had wanted to say: *English village.*
I had wanted to say:
English village a long time ago....
What I had wanted to hear
was the music of flutes and recorders
in a summer garden—
flutes and recorders and tambourines....

What I had wanted to see was light
filtering through the trees
deep in a forest near the sea
where elves and children play together
and adults sip tea
by an enormous ornamented samovar
in solemn conversation
on the nature of the games
the elves & children play....
What I had wanted to write was
love, immortal, laughter, wings....
What I had wanted to do
was to walk forever into a vision
painted by my daughter.
I had wanted her to take me with her there.
I had wanted her
to close the door behind us....

VII

Made of blues and ochers, greens,
made of sunrise and of grass & sky & trees—
Which will be the day
that you remember, child,
when I am only soul-stuff
and can no more enjoy this awkward body
which, despite its ills,
manages to do extraordinary simple things
like walk through heaths of gorse
with you before the others are awake
as the sun comes over
the edge of the earth the ships fall off of
as they tilt on their keels
and roll on the world's last wave. . . .

I remember a day: the rowboat rocked
in the reeds:
my father watched his line. All
the night before we had slept together
in a shack waiting for the dawn.
We didn't talk for hours. He, for once,
was beautifully distracted from
what he always called "the difficult business
of living." There was
no past, there was no future there
in those reeds . . .
                    we were adrift in time,
in timelessness
and no one said we must return—

nor did we sail over any edge of any earth.

Or again: near the house of my childhood
on a street called Glen Echo Drive
there was a tree, an oak,
where my father swung me in a swing—
his long thin fingers
and his firm damp palms on the small of my back
I feel still—
and my bare & grimy feet going up through the leaves!

Mosses grow between his fingers now
and along his palms.
Mosses grow in his mouth & under his arms.
When he finished playing dying
I began. . . .
You gave me pictures
which I held against a wound.
I wrote: *How luminous their rendering* as

You came toward me saying *muzzle, poll, crest,*
withers, loins, croup, dock . . .
As you came saying *snaffle, whip, spurs,*
pommel, cantle, girth.

VIII

And so I try to learn new words
like any child—
I say *flank, hock, heel, hoof;*
I say *fetlock, gaskin, thigh, stifle, sheath.*
I would meet you now
according to my bond. I try to put away
this Ikon which sustained me.

I write *Equitation: Mounting & dismounting.*
Circumspect, I seek
negotiations. I wave my arms
around in frantic circles and insist:
"I'll learn them all"
while you ride off on paths
through fields of gorse and into sunsets
which are not even slightly picturesque—

While you ride off in hurricanes of dust.

—Just one time were three of us together:
father, father-son, and daughter.
We played at something, riding, painting,
poetry, or dying—
it hardly matters what . . .
And at our playing
                    —(while, perhaps,
someone picked a mandolin
and strangers talked about us solemnly
around an ornamental samovar
and sipped their tea)—
our lines of vision crossed
and then we started changing places painfully. . . .

The child is father of the man
but not the child the poet meant.
The child of flesh and blood
and not the ghost of former selves
is father of the man—
The Daughter on the Black Duke of Norfolk
She
is father of the man

The Daughter
Who is Higher, Greater & Completed
She
is father of the man
The Daughter on the Black Duke of Norfolk
The one who made the picture
the one who gave the gift
the one who paved the dead
the one who wore the patch
the one who was Japanese
the one who learned to ride a horse
And Hungers After Herself—

She
is father of the man
The daughter on the Black Duke of Norfolk

The one whose problem was perceptual

The one who rides away

> And the Manual says: *It is interesting to assess the progress*
> *and accuracy of the training by riding a circle on ground upon*
> *which the imprints of the horse's hoofs can be seen. . . .*

(1974–1977)

Part III

Double Invocation
as a Prologue to a Miscellany of Poems
Mostly Written in East Anglia

I

... dRex, dregs, up & out
of the past
by the golden spurs

why not? & drags
him out from under
the bridge

from out of his grave
his marbles intact
and his relics in France

undRex, Edmund Rex
commander Rex
commando and King

and saint! all man
all mundo, myth
and sick of it too

bones in a basket
Abbo's Rex, Ailwin's Rex
and the tourist's:

this is the place
and this is
I truly apologize

only a space I must
clear to begin
and ask for your help

too looming a figure
I know it
but how could I

possibly choose
anyone else
for a guide without

losing my way? Edmund
King and Martyr,
Edmund, King of the bean?

II

A word about Danes is also in order
to make a beginning
to get under way, but who

would put in a word, a good word
for the Danes?
Barbarous heathens you'd say

with curious names like Ubba
& Hingwar & Sweyn
the patricide killer of Blodrand

Sweyn, whose heir was Cnut—I've
spelled it correctly—
Cnut was a King and a Christian

to moot a point.
But I don't know about Danes.
Once I had an *au pair*

and she was a Dane.
I don't think she was a Christian—
large and marvelous tits

I kissed them once in a car
being drunk
though I never saw her Cnut

and one of my closest friends
is a Swede
which is almost a Dane

with a name like Ubba or Sweyn.
Ulfkettle may have com-
manded the army against them in 869.

That would have been against Hingwar.
Did Turchil stand against Sweyn?
I don't know very much about Danes

but O what a lovely girl, my friend,
a calamitous coast,
the wuthering troubles in store!

The Fen Birds' Cry

I

Would you take a caul
along to the sea
it prevents drowning

It shines at birth
prevents
your ship from sinking

On heads of the lucky
a membrane
it makes the solicitor grave

Endows with gift of argument
brings wealth
or would you hold

Hard to the hands of the dead.

II

Would you hold hard to the hands
of the dead
a minute a minute a minute

Or take from the forehead a florin
there where the handywoman
put it the corpse money the florin

Would you have no child for a year
would you take
a caul along to the sea

Prevent drowning prevent
a ship from sinking & make a solicitor
grave would you hold

Hard to the hands of the dead.

Evening Song

Evening: and we
      wait for a train to pass
And my daughter
      says she sees the
Guard's van
      coming round the bend
A quarter of a mile
      or so away.

You mean
      the caboose . . .
I say & she looks happily
      and firmly
At the guard's van
      and pulls
At white cow parsley
      by the fence at the edge
Of the tracks
      that William Carlos
Williams
      in America called
Queen Anne's
      Lace. There's nothing
Royal at all
      about the stuff in Suffolk.

Evening. Laura pulls at
      cow parsley: we
Await the rolling guard's van.
      We live here.

Somewhere in Ohio
    the lantern on the back
Of the world's
    reddest last caboose
Vanishes
    down singing rails
Into the darkness
    of my
        childhood.

Two Ladies

I

So many incorrupt bodies, such
Corrupting times!
Edmund to and fro for years,

Inspected, found intact,
Unburied & unbothered & unblemished
And then, then these ladies

These incorruptible ladies
Like Etheldreda Queen & Sainted Audrey
Earlier than Edmund even

Wearing round her neck a fabled string
Of beads that purpled flesh
Into a fatal tumor that she liked:

She had, she said, been vain.
Daughter of the hypothetical incumbent
Of the ship at Sutton Hoo,

Daughter of the priest who taught her,
Touchy and untouched—
By Tondbert Prince of Fenmen and

By Ecgfrith son of Osway the Northumbrian—
She ruled, queened, twice,
And got sick of it, of royalty, and fled:

Fled to Abbess Eba, solicitous and grave,
Where randy Ecgfrith followed
With his louts who'd leered at her around

The smutty fire inside the great log hall.
Flowering near Ely
Among fowlers, among fishermen & fogs—& bogs—

Famously her pilgrim's staff took root
& that was Etheldreda's Stow.
They say in Etheldreda's Stow today, they *say*—

That water bubbling from her temporary grave
Was Audrey's Spring: & any bauble
There that's worn around the neck's called tawdry.

II

Margery Kempe from Lynn
Would howl and wail "full plenteously"
When told of mirth & pleasures

"Full boisterously" she sobbed
Who was no Wycliffite or Lollard but
Could censure equally

Some bumpkin local reprobate or mighty
Philip Repington and
Greater Arundel upon his Bishop's throne.

Full plenteously, full boisterously
She'd wail: full homely, too!
She was her own Salvation Army band

And drummed and trumpeted vulgarity that
Such as Chesterton would
Understand to be an efficacious pastorale.

Some amanuensis took it down, our first
Biography—be glad! *She* was:
Of plenteous continual weeping by a creature

Who would be the bride of Christ, a pilgrim pure
And not the failed brewer, failed
Miller married to the borough chamberlain

John Kempe that she, said citizens of Lynn,
Pretty clearly was. Contentious;
Weird; she sailed away. The Mamelukes

And Saracens were less impressed with her
Outside the Holy Sepulchre
Than those who'd suffered her for weeks

On board the ship. Said one: a vexèd spirit.
Another: that she'd surfeited on wine.
A third that surely fatal illnesses came on

Like that: *O put her in a heavy sea*
O put her in a little boat
Without a bottom O. Thus, Amanuensis says,

Had each his thoughts. At
York, at Cawood Palace, the Archbishop:
"Woman!—Why, why

Then weepest thou?" And Margery: *Sir, ye*
Shall wish some day
That ye had wept as sore as I!

Dunwich: Winter Visit Alone

for Diana

*"There is presence in what is missing; there is
history in there being so little . . ."*
                                            — HENRY JAMES

Young & younger, we were married here
Where cliffs fall into the sea
And most of the village has
Disappeared, drowning in its leas.
I have not loved you less for that.

And if it is chastening to know
That fishermen catch
Their nets on the bell-towers,
Sunken and singing,
I have not loved you less for that,

Even though I have not loved you
As I might have, if, merchant
Or seaman, I had come here with you
To a safe coast in a good time.
No, I have not loved you less for that.

And knowing well the presences here
From the start, and of absence,
Of history alive, still, in so little,
We face the tides and erosions.
And I will not love you less for that.

No, I will not love you less for that.

Verrucas

The solemn doctor, eyeing painfully
My six verrucas,
Closed the heavy office door—

Well, he said, *we often find in fact*
The skinman doesn't
Do much good, his acids

And his sparks, they
All come back—these warts—
And so we usually

Suggest—and you Americans
Are shocked—
(He looked behind him then)

The local witch. The what?
That's right, he said.
I drove a mile or two and found

Her house. A white witch, certainly,
She smiled a kindly smile
& smoked a caked & gnarled briar pipe.

She counted up verrucas, multiplied,
And tied her knots
In just as many strings

As she would bury, burn, or bless.
I used to use a hunk
Of steak for skin disease, she said,

The method's good. I'd slap
It on a warty cheek or sole, and that
Was that. But what with

Meat so dear and all—you'll understand
We don't use mince! this hex'll
Work for you, all right. Three days!

She packed me hobbling off
& said a spell. I tossed a silver coin
In the bottom of her well.

After the Death of Chekhov

for Bob Hass

Anton Pavlovitch has died
At Badenweiler, a spa
Where doctors had sent him,

A doctor, with his beautiful Olga.
They ship the body to Moscow
Where both of us wait at the station.

This is the difference between us:
You, with Chaliapin & Gorki,
Calm the disorderly crowd

And stick with your man: You
Go off in the proper direction
And weep at the grave of the poet,

While I get confused,
Follow a band of the Tzar's
Which is playing a march

In the cortège of a general
Killed in the Japanese War.
Or, when the two coffins arrive

At the platform together,
One in a car labeled
Oysters, and you understand in

A flash which one is Chekhov's,
This is the difference between us:
You return to your wife and honor

The dead by telling hilarious jokes
About Chaliapin and Gorki, while I am sent
To a spa in the car labeled *Oysters*.

You Measure John

for Diana, at work in the Fitzwilliam

For posterity you measure John.
For the catalogue
you measure with a tape
his works
and recognize yourself as woman
among women
in the life of this man John, his death.

You measure for the catalogue
the pictures
and their frames
thinking of the others
measuring his need
measuring his pride (who could not
please himself)
measuring his gypsy caravans of children
as he went away to paint, badly,
the famous and the rich.

No, you do not like Augustus John.
Measuring the thickness
of a new biography you offer me
I think—
not. You tell it simply
and with no embellishments yourself.
It is an old story:
some man damages the lives of women
who would love him.
There are various excuses.
One is art.

My Youngest Daughter: Running
Toward an English Village Church

Sunday, then. In Trumpington. And nearby bells.
My daughter runs among the village graves
this foggy January morning of her early youth
as I lie late in bed
and watch her from my window.

I know she holds her breath.
Superstitious, she'll hold it till she passes by
the final marker near the door & disappears inside.
If you breathe in cemeteries
you inhale evil spirits!
What do you inhale when you breathe in stony
churches or in bedrooms where you wake alone
and realize you cannot tell
your child's superstition from her faith?

Beyond the church, a village green, a meadow,
the pleasures and the picnics
of next spring. I tell her
not to hold her breath in graveyards.
Watching her red coat become a gaudy blur
against the brilliant hoarfrost,
I realize I'm holding mine.

Mark Twain in the Fens

I

Not the trip of 1872
when fame first fanned an Anglophilia
and glory burst from every side
upon him—
And not the trip of 1879
when he howled for *real coffee,*
corn bread, good roast beef
with taste to it.

The last trip; the exile & the debts.

Thish-yer Smiley had a yeller
one-eyed cow that didn't have no tail . . .
At Brandon Creek, Ship Inn.
They bring him real coffee, good
roast beef with taste to it.

II

      Recently got up
by him as Joan of Arc,
his eldest daughter once had fled
the Bryn Mawr auditorium—
meningitis all but creeping
up her spine—

He told them all a tingler,
having sworn to her he wouldn't,
called *The Golden Arm.*

Death made real by hers?
and deathless tales
a part of blame? *My fault, my fault—*
And this: *I'll pay*
though still he dreams each night
about his miracle-working
machine, the Paige Typesetter,
his Dark Angel of print.

III

Thish-yer Smiley had a yeller
one-eyed cow that didn't have no tail . . .

No one writes it down
or sets it up in type. It is the last
he is going to tell.

It is all over with him. It's
begun. All night long
he tells and tells and tells.

Paul Verlaine in Lincolnshire

I

For a while he had that famous friendship.
But what's inspired debauchery
and manic vision
to illuminations from the English hymnal?
Keble's stanzas? Wesley's? Stanzas
by good Bishop Ken?
Ô mon Dieu, vous m'avez blessé d' amour.

For indulgence, there was Tennyson.
He walked to Boston from the grammar school
in Stickney to confess.

II

And wrote *Sagesse* there in Lincolnshire.
And went to chapel,
and taught the ugly boys finesse.
He had been condemned to death,
he boasted, in the Siege
of Paris . . .
        Colonel Grantham and
the credulous headmaster
listened to the story
of his clever rescue by Thiers. . . .

Even in the hands of Debussy, Fauré,
the Catholic *lied* Verlainian would sing
the strangest nonconformist airs.

Ô mon Dieu, vous m'avez blessé d'amour.

III

And to proper Mallarmé he wrote
about the absinthe: *I'd still take it
with sugar.* . . .
The school record books
do not suggest
that he excelled at rugger.

O there were many rhymes—
But he was on his best behavior,
pious, calm, bourgeois.
The peaceful English countryside
acted on his conscience
like a rudder.

Ô mon Dieu, vous m'avez, blessé d'amour.

Words for Sir Thomas Browne

I

If melancholy is a sadness with no reasonable cause,
your son Tom's death at sea produced in you a grief

and not a melancholy. You would define, define again,
whose testimony helped convict, in 1655,

two witches in the court of Matthew Hale. Gentle man,
they hung on Suffolk gallows till they died.

You bore no kind of malice towards them, either one,
and you studied to avoid all controversy always.

But if no witches did the Devil's work, it followed
that no works were done among us by the Spirits,

and from that, no doubt "obliquely," that the hierarchy
of creation would collapse & neither New Philosophy

nor love could save the soul of your young Tom
who read & praised the pagans on his ship *whose noble*

straynes, you thought, *may well affect a generous mind.*
Amazed at *those audacities, which durst be nothing,*

and return into their Chaos once again, you recommended
orthodoxy and you testified for Matthew Hale.

II

Death was occupation and preoccupation both in Norwich
where you practiced medicine, exploded vulgar errors,

contemplated cinerary urns. You did not *secretly implore
& wish for plagues, rejoyce at famines*, or *revolve*

ephemerides in expectation of malignant aspects & eclipses
like certain others of your trade. Your prayers

went with the husbandmans, desiring *everything in proper
season, that neither men nor times be out of temper.*

But they were deeply & profoundly out of temper, the men
and times in your extraordinary time. New Science

studied to discern the cause and was itself part cause
and part effect. Love got on with its peculiar,

frail, sublunary affairs: and though you'd be *content that
we might procreate like trees without conjunction,*

husbands awkwardly attended to their husbandry, and you
yourself begot a dozen saplings. Of the seven who survived,

Edward was the firstborn and the doctor, but Tom was your
particular delight—& like to make, you thought, at once

a navigator & a scholar on that ship of Captain Brookes—
and like to take the draughts of all things strange.

III

Pythagoras and Lucan, Epicurus too: he took the draughts
of these and dwelt on noble suicides, on transmigrations,

and on souls that dwelt in circuits of the moon or souls
eternally annihilated in eternal night.

Audacious draughts: they'd make a generous mind so drunk
it might conceive itself invaded by the speech of Vulteius

and urge, in some engagement where a Netherlandish Pompey
stole the victory & then prevented honorable escape,

the sober Roman medicine you feared. How did Thomas die?
If he fell upon his sword, or, lost to Admiral Kempthorne,

lit a powder keg and blew his ship to kingdom come,
we never heard. If some malefic doctor set about to loose

a plague, or grinning crones beside a rocky coast at dawn
spun almanacks and made a storm, you never said.

You did your work: you sought to cure the ill & comforted
the dying, you strangled mice and chickens on your

kitchen scales to see if *weight increaseth when the vital
spirits flee,* you demonstrated that the elephant

indeed has joints, that beavers do not ever *in extremity
bite off their stones,* that no bear brings her

young into the world *informus and unshapen* to fashion them
by licking with her tongue, that Eve & Adam had no navels

and that Jesus wore (a Nazerite by birth) short hair.
Often you returned to your initial, fundamental ground:

Whatever impulse be unlocked by Lucan's strains, whatever
operation be insinuated in us when, Satanic,

we're inhabited by arguments which say *necessity* or *chance*
or *fate*, a lucid sense of order could, you thought,

when mixed in some alembic with humility & grace, explain
and purge away (though witches must, alas, be hanged).

IV

As though the soul of one man passed into another,
opinions, after certain revolutions, do find men & minds

like those that first begat them.

Staring fixedly at Tom's
last letter in your hand, thinking of that trial where

one alleged his chimney had been cursed & yet another that
his cart had been bewitched and also all his geese,

you well might suddenly embrace that sweet & generous heresy
that tempted you when you were young: that all are saved—

yourself & Tom, those witches in the court of Matthew Hale,
Epicurus, Lucan & Pythagoras, cruel doctors who revolve

ephemerides, husbands who attend to husbandry, sons and
daughters, brothers aunts & sisters, wives.

And yet you said: *God saves whom he will* . . .
and thought the wretched women damned at Edmund's bury.

And thought you heard Tom's ship explode at sea.

Lines for the Gentlemen

I

1667. And on Landguard beach, 1000 Dutch.
That was the last invasion.
Afterwards, 1753–66,
Governor Thicknesse, thank you, defending, sir.
(And plenty of out-of-work sailors)

II

And as with piracy, there's honour in it.
And not just honour among thieves—
A rising class will not, they'd tell you,
be put down. Custom?
                    Brandy! tea, wool, rum,
just name it—
So the word gets round. Someone's
had the pox, someone's
had the plague. All's free trade
at certain cottages where rumoured illnesses
or rumoured ghosts
keep all but customers away—

Laces for a lady; letters for a spy
And watch the wall, my darling, while the
    Gentlemen go by.

III

This one watched the wall; that one
closed his eyes.
The headless gunner walked on the embankment.

A crescent moon rose smartly from behind
the nasty gibbet. There are
voices in the back room of The Crown—

and Mr Plumer, MP from Appleby,
speaking in the House
and saying ALL IMPROVEMENT OF THE LAND

HAS BEEN SUSPENDED
while the Parson whispers to his wife
the wages of gin

for our duties
and hides the three enormous tubs
beneath the altar cloth.

4,000,000 gallons of booze are flowing
into England! (Three slow
cutters chasing one fast swipe.)

The publican
has put the spotsmen all to sleep.
Bright lights are flashing

down the Orwell and the Alde.

From a Visit to Dalmatia, 1978

I

Korčula is oleander, cypresses & twisted
fig trees; Korčula is stones —
Lemon trees and stones. Quick mirages
above the stones & olive groves:
Shaky vineyard walls of broken stones and

Stones that must be gathered, piled up
before the shallow roots will
take a tenuous hold
in sandy earth: And shallow stony graves
for Partisan or priest, invader.

Limestone & limestone rock in hills
around Lumbarda, limeface of Sveti Ilija
after Orebić:
                Rockslides and
washed out roads, karst —
a landscape that will break you on its back
or make a sculptor of you —

Lozica, Kršinić, Ivan Jurjević-Knez.

II

Or if not a sculptor then a fisherman.
Or, it would have once.

       Looking at the empty streets
at noon, Toni Bernidić
tells me it's the woist and hottest
day so far in June—he learned
his English in Brooklyn
during the war—
But his house is cool, and so
are the wines: Grk, Pošip, Dingač. . . .
He tells me of the wooden ships
he built, each one taking
him a year: but well made, well made—
The work, he says,
was heavy—pointing to his tools.

Now he has no work: the island's
income is from tourists
and the flushed young men who'd once
have been apprentices
sport their *Atlas* badges, ride their
scooters to the Park or Marco Polo
or the Bon Repos
and show their muscles to the breezy
blue-eyed girls
whose wealthy fathers order loudly
wiener schnitzel

wienerschnitzel and stones.

Friendship

One day I do you a good turn. Then
You do me *two* good turns.
I am pleased by that & say so the next day.

You break the lead in your pencil.
I loan you mine.
You give me an expensive fountain pen.

I play you a recording of The Modern Jazz Quartet.
Though you like Milt Jackson's vibes, you
Take me to *The Ring* at Covent Garden after which

We introduce each other to our wives.
My wife teaches your wife how to cook fondues.
Your wife teaches my wife how to live.

I dedicate my book to you & you are moved.
You make a character of me in yours:
It is singled out for praise by the reviewers.

I give my mistress to your loyalest disciple.
Claiming he is bored with her, you have
The wench returned; her skills are much improved.

When I sing my secret lute song about mountains,
You take me to the mountains
In your car: You have a cabin there

Where after drinks we agree to a primitive contest.
Preparing for it, you
Scar your face grotesquely with a razor blade.

Upon return, I burn for you my manuscript.
For me you smash your files. I wreck my mother's house.
You wreck your only daughter's mind.

In the end, I write a letter saying:
I forgive you. But you do not write back.
It is now the time for silence.

For we are friends. We love each other very much.

Agape

(after the poem by César Vallejo)

I won't say anyone comes here and asks.
They haven't this afternoon
Asked me for anything much. Nothing!

Not one leper presented himself.
I haven't today
Kissed my quota of sores.

In so fine a parading of lights, I haven't
Seen a single burial flower.
Lord, Lord: I've died so little today,

I'm sorry, forgive me. Everybody goes by
But nobody asks for a thing.
Mal, mal in my hands, like a *cosa ajena.*

If you've mislaid it it's here!
Well, I've gone to the door & I've shouted.
How many doors get slammed in my face!

Something *ajeno ajeno* roots in my soul
And I don't tell you somebody comes here & asks.
Lord, Lord: I've died so little today.

Brandon, Breckland: The Flint Knappers

(after a chapter in Julian Tennyson's Suffolk Scene)

The Forestry Commission was about to plant
the Breckland on the day young Julian Tennyson

visited the Edwardses, last knappers of Brandon.
Because some tribes in Central Africa

hadn't hear about percussion caps
there still was business for the craftsmen

that supplied the flint for Wellington
and watched the plovers & the curlews dip at home.

Alien, the Breckland seemed as sinister & desolate
to Tennyson as 1938, the stark flint cottages

all shining darkly in reflecting pools
of stone and dusty sorrel, riding in the ragwort

and the bugloss, or jutting out of bracken,
heather, thin brown grass.

Wheatears, stonechats, whinchats, pipits—
all in the same still air—

and Julian, once a Suffolk countryman's Huck Finn,
feeling terrors coming on him

now at twenty-three, feeling *loosed in some
primeval, flat and limitless arena*—

leagues and leagues and leagues of it, he wrote,
severed from the rest of England.

Brandon on the Little Ouse was a relief from that,
though still in Breckland.

Malting, watermeadows, fine old bridge —
as lovely a corner as any I have found in Suffolk.

The elder Edwards, coughing, takes him
in his workshop, shuts the door, and points:

topstone, wallstone, floorstone chips
from Lingheath Common quarry, ornaments & tinders,

flints for muskets, carbines, pistols —
quartered first, then flaked and knapped with

pointed hammer on a flattened rod of iron.
When the headmen learn about percussion caps

the shows all over, Edwards said.
And anyway we've not got one apprentice

and the quarrier's retired. It would die with him,
his art, these mysteries of Breckland.

Meanwhile Tennyson looks on amazed
as Edwards bevels edges, hammers, hammers, talks:

I did it on the radio into a microphone, I
did it on the BBC before the news.

There are reports. Off in Central Africa
sprawls a man who feels of a sudden loosed in some

primeval flat and limitless arena—
leagues and league and leagues of it, he thinks

in his delirium. There is a flight of birds.
On Berner's green: an Air Ministry bombing-ground;

here the Forestry Commission will plant firs.
Badgers and foxes, jays and crows

will populate the land the curlews flee, *and when
the Old Guard fell before great Wellington*

England sang the knappers of the Brandon flints!
It is the year of Munich. Tennyson will die

in Burma from a piece of shrapnel the size of any
smallish hag-stone he'd have found

among discarded chips on Edwards' dusty floor
and which his copy of George Borrow

pressing pages from a manuscript of *In Memoriam*
will not deflect. Reflected in his book,

an Indian summer. Ice will one day lift
the Blaxhall Stone itself as far as Brandon moor.

59 Lines Assembled Quickly
Sitting on a Wall Near the Reconstruction
of the Lady Juliana's Cell

Heavily   heavily
hidden away—

the door is
barred & barred   and

singing
veni creator

spiritus "a service
of Enclosure"

& the cell
is consecrated

and the door
is barred   and

singing
veni creator

spiritus you have
a window on

the church you have
a window on

the world
and appearances

and revel-
lations   visions!

"showings"
to a soul *that*

cowde
no letter: cowde—

could, cloud
no cloud or cold

unknowing sin
is what

there loud? or
quiet sin is what

behoved? or is
behovable

il convient que
le péché

existe: le péché is
serviceable

what is
an anchorhold what is

an anchoress
the Lady Juliana's

one re-
corded visit from the

frenzied Margerie Kempe
as praise

& praise & gesture
I prefer

to Juliana's
Kemp's

the *other* Kemp's
Will Kemp's

who Morris-danced
from London

days   on days
from London

Kemp's who
lept!   immortally

this Norwich wall

26 June 1381/1977

I NORTH WALSHAM: THE FIELDS

And he, Despenser, tried to keep hold
Of the dyer's head

As the crowd of them, gawkers
& priests, tinkers & tailors & wastrels

(Gentry too, thinking already: *reredos!*
A gift for him, a

Presentiment) lurched along
With the horsecart off to the place

Of undoing, Lidster's undoing who'd heard—
Who'd heard of *The Kynges*

Son who'd paye for al,
The mullere who'd ygrounde smal—but

Was paying himself,
Tied by a foot with the same rope

That they'd hang him with, after
The drawing. And he

Henry Despenser, the Bishop "Lespenser"—
miles amatus, boni pastoris mens,

For so it says on his brass—
Hopping behind the cart like a toad,

The cart they dragged the dyer behind
For that was the law:

To be dragged to the place of undoing.
This, however, was extra:

The Bishop himself coddling your head
In his skirts

And you "The King of the Commons,"
"The Idol of Norfolk"

Whose bell had been rung
By Ball and Tyler and Straw. Oh

This dispenser of justice was special,
sui generis the man who

Had caught you, tried you, confessed you,
The man who would hang you

See you in quarters, one for each of
The earth's: hopping

Behind the cart like a toad . . .
And reaching out for your head   which

Aoi!   he'd drop on a cobble a cobble
a cobble and *there*

Then catch it up again, mother it back
In his apron, your head

Like an apple or melon or globe. Where,
Where did you travel, where

Did you think you could go—
The two of you, then, staff, of one, life?

II St Luke's Chapel, Norwich Cathedral

We look at the reredos, the retables.
Of course the "subject"

Is "Christ." . . . But the blood & the power
That steadied the hand

And shook the knees and the wits of the
Master from Norwich—*that*

Was the blood and the power of Dyer
And Bishop, of Lidster

And Henry Despenser. Behind me somebody
Mumbles the word *chiliastic.*

His fellow-tourist says, looking hard: it's
Absolutely fantastic!

The five panels escaped the smashing
Of Cromwell. The five

Scenes from the Passion here are restored.
And we may embrace

The arcana, study
The photomicrographic specifics:

A patient lady explains: *malachite,*
Azurite: And the head of Christ is restored!

The rotten wood is restored: the order
Is restored. *Israelite,*

Trotskyite. Edmund Burke said of the famous
Rhyme: *it rhymes!* And also: *a sapient*

Maxim: When Adam delved and Eve span, who
Was then the gentle man?

Nobody knows what Lidster said, but that's
What he heard: *The Kynges son schal*

Paye for al
The mullere hath ygrounde smal—and

Paid it himself,
Tied by a foot with the same rope

They'd etcetera. *Spin:*
The painting and the restoration

Are brilliantly done. *Delve:* the revolt
Alas was untimely—even Engels

Would say so—and Henry Despenser's work
Was brilliantly done—

And us with our heads still on our necks?
With books in our laps,

Stupid or giddy, gawking—
Us with the eyes still in their sockets

And tongues still in our mouths—
Where do we travel, where

Do we think we can go—
All of us now, staff, of one, life?

On the Death of Benjamin Britten

Operas! A feast for burghers, said Adorno.
And of your work: The apotheosis
Of meagerness, a kind of fast. That's
A cruel case against you
And it may have weight, in time.
But let's call meagerness
Economy today
And call the bourgeoisie the people
Who like me have (barely) what it costs
To listen and who like to hear
These songs, but who will pay a price.
Economies of living soon enough
Make meager even music of the spheres!
To be of use, you said.
Directly and deliberately I write
For human beings. And not
Posterity—for which the general outlook
Isn't very bright.

A tenor mourns. And you lie down in Aldeburgh
One last time. But you have work to do
In spite of what the two of us have said.
A tenor sings. When you
Get out there over the horizon
This December morning with the likes
Of Peter Grimes,
Row your shining boat ashore
And be extravagant in song:
Leave economy to the ungrateful living
Who will need it, whose Justice
And whose History have multiplied unendingly
Expenses by Apotheoses by Sublimes.

An East Anglian Diptych

in memoriam Robert Duncan and David Jones

LEY LINES

I

. . . & flint by salt by clay
by sunrise and by sunset
and at equinox, by equinox,

these routes, these
lines were drawn, are drawn,
(force by source of sun)

The dowser leans by Dod-man's
ley alignment and
against some oak by water now.

II

By flint: the tools
By salt: the meats
By clay: the rounded pots

Along the lines, by sun-
rise & by sunset
and at equinox, by equinox,

The Dod-man's sighting staves,
one in each hand, is it,
of that scoured long chalk man?

III

Past Tom Paine's house behind the puddingstone
and castle there aligned
strategically along the Icknield way

Beyond the Gallows Hill
beside the Thetford tracks to Brandon
down the Harling Drove

Across the Brickkiln Farm to Bromehill Cottage
& below the tumuli before
the rabbit warrens and top hats . . .

Some burials, some dead,
and here their flinted offerings.
Seven antler picks,

A phallus made of chalk,
a Venus (did they call her yet Epona?)
and a tallow lamp . . .

Beltane fire line forty miles long?
Conflagration's law where energy's electric
down the *herepath*

if *Belus* is spelt *Bel* . . .

~

No bronze until the Beakers.
No phosphorous lucifers until, say, 1832.
Toe holes, ropes allowed descent

for wall stone you could antler out,
shovel with a shoulder bone—
Floor stone you would crawl for . . .

Between the galleries, burrows
narrow as a birth canal, as dark,
where some half-blinded Neolith first

nudged the Brandon Blacks & passed
those flints as far down time as Waterloo.
Weapons, tools. Ornaments as well.

Flushwork on Long Melford Church.
Flint flake Galleting on Norfolk Guildhall.
Jags by thousands of the calcined stones

for Queen Victoria's potteries.
Strike-a-lights required on Maundy Thursday still—
oldest flints ignite a young god's Pascal wick,

But first an edge to cut away the underbrush
down ley lines
long before the Beakers and their bronze.

IV

Ten days, twelve chapters, and the young man soon to die at Arras
finishes his book, his thirtieth or so, on the Icknield way. It's mostly
about walking. He walks from Thetford where he thinks the Way
begins coming from the Norfolk ports across the River Thet and
Little Ouse. He's melancholy. The times are difficult, he's poor, he'd
rather be a poet, his wife is desperate for his company, his children
miss him too, a war is coming on, and anyway, he's melancholy by
nature. He has a friend who tries to show him how to turn his
prose to verse. He'll have two years to do just that before he dies
on Easter Monday, 1917.

But now he walks and writes. It is a job. They pay you for these
nature books, these evocations, all this naming you can do along
the road and through the villages and over all the dykes. They'll
buy your eye even if they're deaf to all this balancing of consonants
and vowels. He's melancholy. He doesn't really want to take this
walk. He does it for the money. The times are difficult, he's poor,
he'd rather be a poet, his wife is desperate for his company, his chil-
dren miss him too, a war is coming on. Still,

It's better on a path than on a pavement.
It's better on the road than in a town.
It's better all alone to walk off melancholy
than to poison a companionable air
(or to stare out of a muddy trench in France.)

Home, returned on leave, exhausted,
bored by prose he's published only months before
and talking with a friend who'll ask:
And what are you fighting for over there?

he'll pick a pinch of earth up off the path
they're walking and say: *This!*
For this, he'll say.
This This This

For

    this

     ~

This King Belinus was especially careful
to proclaim that cities
and the highways that led unto them

would have the peace
Dunwello had established in his time.
But no one seemed to know

the rules or lines whereby the boundaries
of the roads had been determined.
Neither Geoffrey, who, saying that about

Belinus in his book then consults the works
of Gildas, nor Gildas either,
nor Nennius himself in *Historia Brittonum.*

Before Belinus paved the road to "Hamo's Port"
with stone and mortar as he paved
Foss Way and Watling Street, walkers who

brought flint, brought salt, brought clay,
paved the way in footprints over peat
and grasses with their animals before them

or behind. *By flint:* the tools;
By salt: the meats; *by clay:* the rounded pots.
By ley lines, flint and clay and salt

by sunrise and by sunset
and at equinox, by equinox, these routes,
these lines were drawn

(but no one seemed to know the rules
whereby the boundaries
of the roads had been determined)

force by source of sun.

    V

They leaned into the journey,
east to west,
beyond Grimes Graves and through

the place that would be Thetford.
For every dragon heard to have been slain,
they found a standing stone. . . .

Beside the Hill of Helith and then
along the river Lark
they left their weapons and their coins,

wondered at the headless rider
riding on the muddy banks. Cautious, curious
at the Swales tumulus, at

barrows north of Chippenham, they guessed
fine Wessex bronze lay gleaming
in the buried dagger there . . . and aged (grew young),

passed by Burwell church, passed by
Burwell castle too, spoke
of Anna and of Etheldreda, queen and saint,

at Exing, saw the horses race along
by Devil's Ditch to Reach, gallop through
the sainfoin which they gathered

in their hands as stone aligned with stone,
church with church, holy well
with holy well, pylon (in the end) with pylon.

Counting *one five four: four seven four:
four eight six* at Whittlesford,
brides among them turned their heads

to gaze at Golliwog, Shiela-na-gig.
Whose giggle, then, this
gog-eyed goggle goddess ogling back

above the portal near the Wandlebury
Gogmagog? *By air:* the zodiac;
By fire: the dragon path; *by earth:*

the tumulus, the barrow and the grave.
East to west
they leaned into the journey where

the dowser leans by Dod-man's
ley alignment and
against some oak by water now.

RIVERS

I

By touch: his twig reveals the waters,
his sounding rod bites into chalk.
Matrona, Bel and Wandil gather in the mist

upon the hillside, lean into the journey:
moon by sun against the darkness,
sun by moon against the giant with a sword.

By air: the signal from the Gogmagogs
to zodiacs at Edmund's Bury and Nuthamstead.
Knight to knight come forth. By air

the still response: the bull, the lion;
the eagle & the bear. If Wandil stole the spring,
spread his frost along the ley lines,

now he strides as Gemini across the sky.
(Not two children, not two goats,
but eyes of Wandil rain down geminids

where ancient Dod-men lie. . . .)

II

By water now. Along the Lark to Bury
where by air the constellations
blaze down on these figures born of earth.

Was it before Beodricsworth became
Saint Edmund's town & shrine
that Sigebert's forebears paced off zodiacs

from Abbots Bridge to Stoke-by-Claire
discerned as fit propitiation still
by him who led the garlanded white bull

to its oblation for the barren girl
between imposing portals
of the Benedictine Abbey on the Lark?

By rivers then. Along this quiet one
past Bury where it forms
the tail of Sagittarius and on by sting

of Scorpio, by tribute and by tributary,
portaging on over Virgo
north of Shimpling to Chad Brook. . . .

Where the Stour flows by Long Melford
they leaned into their journey, rowed along
the belly of the Lion close by Clare.

If Wandil gestured to the west, they
travelled east toward Harwich, backs against
the morning sun, oars against the tide.

Underbrush along the banks at first
held only otters, then at Mysteleigh solemn men
sat fishing, men knelt making salt;

at Manningtree, a single lighter hauled
the heavy stones up shallow higher reaches
where a mason waited with his tools

and visions of a chancel in his brain.
Stoke and Wilford built their low stone bridges then;
other towns built locks; local wool

brought bricks and lime and coal.
West to east, they met the horse-drawn barges,
passed young woodsmen felling trees

to build the *Thorn,* the *Syren* and the *Terpsichore.*
Lark by Stour by Orwell; Scorpio
by Lion. Moon by sun against the darkness.

Sun by moon. A giant with a sword. . . .

III

Or with a ship. A *Syren* or a *Terpsichore.* And if a giant, then a giant
metamorphosed over time. The man who'll six years later paint
the *Hay Wain* may not know his river rises as a tiny brook east of
the Chilterns in the Gogmagogs. And yet he feels the giant in it,
yet he knows its gods. Today he finishes his sketch of Flatford Mill
—the mill itself, the locks, the barge and bargemen, and the
small distracted barefoot boy on his horse. He'll work it up in
1817 for the Academy and no one will complain that it lacks
finish. The sketch itself is rough. He adds an ash—his favorite tree
—some elms, a broken oak. He shades in clouds he's come to
study with a meteorologist's precision. Then he shuts the sketch
book and trudges off toward Dedham, marking in his mind the

river's fringe of willowherb and reed, the rising heron and the
darting snipe and redshank in the sky....

He wants to marry Charles Bicknell's daughter. He wants to paint
this river and these shimmering green fields. He doesn't want to
quarrel with Charles Bicknell, with the rector of his village, or
with Bonaparte. And he doesn't want to paint for money portraits
of the rich or of their homes: Malvern Hall, Petworth House, East
Bergholt. The ships that followed *Thorn* on down the slips at
Mistly shipyards belched a thousand years of Beltane fire at
French sails on the Nile. Martello towers rose at Shotley and at
Walton Ferry ... But here and now it's quiet, he thinks. Here and
now it's peaceful and the air is pure ...

It's better to paint rivers than great houses.
It's better to be married than alone.
It's better with companionship to sit through winter nights
remembering the Stour in springtime
(or a cousin lying face-down in the mud at Waterloo).

Here, returned from London, nervous and annoyed,
bored by portraits that he's painted only months before
and talking to a friend who asks:
And what are you drawing landscapes for out here?

he picks a pinch of earth up off the path
they're walking and says *This!*
For this, he says.
This This This
For

    this

     ~

This other ryver called of old time
Fromus maketh his beginning
near to Framlingham and then descendeth

close by Marlesford and so
southeast of Farnham entertayneth yet
another ryver called the Gleme

which cometh out from Rendlesham
thus passing forth to Snapebridge and
contriving then his course to Yken

dedicates himself into the sea
not very far away from where the Stour & Orwell
run together into Harwich harbour.

Framlingham: Framela's people: strangers on
the Fromus before Fromus became Alde.
Folk who'd become burgen-holders paying 5d tax.

On the bluff above the mere the Bigods' castle
glowers: Henry's caste glowers back
from Orford. Herrings, cereals, pottery from

Staverton passed through the town, began a journey
inland or a journey to the coast.
Scratchings on the nave in Parham church

show navigable reaches: ships of the little draft
came all the way from Normandy past
Orford, Sloughden, Iken, down this stream

that flows
into a pipe below a petrol station

now

    IV

        ... Men will number
what they value most
in wills: 'To Robert Cook my scalbote,

my anchor and the things belonging to it and
my spurling bote: to George Clare
my fysher, fartle, makerel nets & warropes:

To John Weylonde: A manfare of haryngnetts:
capstaynes, skewers & my sparlyng netts
that hangeth in the low to the sea this yere

and when the sparlyngfare is done the netts
schal then be partyd to my children:
Thomas, Christopher, Erasmus: ships belonging

to the havyn to be sold at Aldeburgh church.'
The men who made the wills were fishermen;
The others built their boats along these shores ...

or sold them victuals, or worked upon the land,
or herded sheep, kept inns, cut
the timber, prayed in church & monastery, wept

impressed at sea, took up piracy and smuggling,
made the malt that made the ale they drank,
organized themselves in unions, and were hanged.

By 1850 photographs appear to show us
what they looked like outside Newton Garrett's
maltings or beside their barges loading

at Snape quay. John Felgate, shipwright, has
no teeth and wears a cap of moleskins;
his son, standing by a dinghy, has a thick

mustache, a threadbare coat, & a determined gaze.
Jack Ward, skipper of the *Gladys*, smiles;
his heavy begrimed turtleneck presses up against

his graying whiskers and his wide square chin.
The carpenters, Alfred Andrews & his son,
look almost well-to-do beside the shipwrights;

the younger Andrews wears a tie, a waistcoat,
and a golden chain while sawing timber for a rudder
or a boom; Howell and Chatten, maltsters,

hold their massive wooden shovels, handles down,
and slop about in canvas boots. Their rugged faces
look like copper pennies in a winter sun.

If we could hear them speak we'd doubtless hear
them say how *chance-times a sloe-wind*
brings old Tabbler Cable back to that same mawther

who'd 'im *clapper-clawed* or hear them laugh about
the crones who *couldn't sculpt the roots*
out as they got no teeth. The carter thakketh his hors

upon the croupe and jumps up in his wagon.
He's off to town. The men who work the maltings
and the bargemen line up for their pay.

The bird that flies above them angling toward
the Orford Ness they call a *mavis;*
by the time it reaches sprawling spider-webs

of early-warning radar nets it's lost its name,
and anyone at Chantry Point
looking with binoculars for avocets or curlews

would only see, if it passed by, a thrush.
Along the ley-alignment point
at Sizewell, Beltane fires in the reactor

are contained by water drained out of the sea.

        V

        . . . But that the salt sea of say A.D. 500
should be drained from Deben marshes
that the land be sweet for corn and cattle . . .

That the river rising beyond Sutton, beyond
Woodbridge wait out flood & tide
for Norman engineers and then the Dutch,

for every local Fosdike, every local Waller
who might learn the warping
and the inning, reclaim with bank & seawall

or with sluice & gutter marshes then defended
by the reeves of Walton and
the men of Melton who might write: *lately salt,*

now fresh ... That would take some time.
Some time, too, before the signals flash from
castle cresset, lucomb, lighthouse

or Martello tower up and down the coast
from Goseford to the Alde. No
early warnings here where everything's surprise.

South to north, they leaned into the journey,
rounded Landguard Point and
passed by Walton Castle, sailing with the tide

across the sand bar, steersman hugging
his athwartship tiller, small rain
in the oarsmen's eyes, wind across the stern.

Beyond the sandy heathland, the turf & bracken
over which they'd lug a ship the
size of this one to be buried as a cenotaph—

with coins from Usson-du-Poitou, a golden helmet,
maple lyre, & stone sceptre carved
with eight stern faces and a thin bronze stag

mounted on its delicate iron ring—
they reached the pools they sought and, anchoring
off mud flats, felled the trees,

built their timber halls beyond abandoned villas,
stayed at Hemley, Hatchley, Trimley,
called the river that they sailed "the deep one."

They'd say they lived in *Middanyeard,* where *haeleth*
under heofenum: they found themselves
between two seas . . . (the hero of their poem the sun).

Before them, Celts and Roman legions.
After them the Viking raids.
After them the Norman engineers and Flemish traders.

Before them, the single salters squatting
on the mud, the long walk for flints
along the Icknield way. After them the excavation

of the buried ship. . . .

      ~

    Extensio. Eastern point
north of Southwold on the Easton Ness, now lost.
Portus Adurni. Was the Deben called Adurnus

by the Latins here and on the Alde?
Harbour, temperate climate, sheltered creeks—
and vines growing high above the cliffs.

Counts of the Saxon Shore constructed here
their fortress where they failed to hold the tide
against the kin of those first called

by Vortigern to fight his wars against the Picts.
(St. Alban's first cartographer
would clearly mark his map: *Angulus Anglie* . . .)

Around the corner, then, and up the river
with the driftwood & the tide. Buoyed and beaconed,
spits and banks first marked with small

bouquets of yellow broom display their
angled emblems: Bowships beacon, Middleground,
Upper Waldringfield and Lower Ham,

Jack Rush beacon, Crimmy Moore, Horse Buoy.
If Edward were to anchor here
along the Kingsfleet, who but the Archbishop

might come sailing smartly out of Shotley
as the king, shining like some Helith, went to meet him
round into the Stour? On board the *Thomas,*

in a western wind, the Goseford ships impressed
for service, the power upon them
& Calais in fear, they'd break up the Great Seal.

So Wandil on the Stour gestures gravely
to the Wandil on the Gogmagogs. Against him lean
the sun & moon while all about him

widdershins there turns a circle of the dancers
who will help achieve the spring
as every ley south-east of Thetford Castle Mound

lines up along the tumuli and standing stones
to pass through places named for Bel
or Belus out to Walton on the northern Sea. . . .

Beyond the Roman camp, the Saxon mound.
Beyond the Saxon mound the Viking
outpost in the Celtic forest with its secret paths.

Along the paths, the route to tributaries,
creeks, the sweetest hidden wells. Above the wells
a dowser with his twig, a Dod-man

with his sighting staves. . . .

　　　　～'

　　　who walks along the concrete wall,
and feels the fresh salt air,
and watches small yachts ply the quiet river

at high tide. Red sails, blue.
And bright white hulls. Woodbridge Sunday sailors
tack and jibe . . .

Alde by Stour by Deben. Ship by Saxon shore.
Cattle, corn by sea wall.
Dod-man, dowser, dapple of reflected cloud.

Part IV

Rhododendron

Several years ago, you planted
near my study window something green.
Today I notice it, not just green,

but blazing red-in-green exactly
like the rhododendron it turned out
to be when you said: *Look!*

My rhododendron's flowering.
As usual, I had never asked, had
never noticed, would not have

had an answer if our daughter or
her friend had said a day ago: *And that?*
Just what is that? It's something green,

I'd have had to say, *that your mother*
planted there, some kind of flower
that hasn't flowered yet, although

she planted it three years ago.
It's the word itself, I think, that's
made it flower, and your saying it.

The winter's not been easy, and the
spring's been slow. I stared at long white
papers full of emptiness and loss

as one might stare at rows of narrow
gardens full of snow. The words
have not come easily, have not come well.

Easily, you tell me, stepping through
the door: *Look! my rhododendron's
flowering.* . . . And it is, and it does.

Not having read a single fairy tale

for a long long time
because my children are now grown,
I buy a book of them for the child of friends
and later get caught up in it alone
waiting nervously beside the phone
for word of an adult.

Once there was a cat
who made acquaintance of a rat.
There was a peasant once
who drove his oxen with a heavy load of wood.
An ugly fisherman lived with an ugly wife
in an ugly shack beside the heaving sea.
A man was rich, another man was poor.
A father called his children in before him.
Once there was a little girl
whose mother and father had died.
Once there was a witch.

Time passes. It is late.
Outdoors the wind is howling, and it rains.
My beard turns gray and
grows between my legs, grows
across the carpet, down the basement stairs.
The house creaks. The globe
spins off its axis, smashes on the floor.

The telephone is ringing off the hook.
My daughter is all right.

For William and Teresa

Everything to be endured

you said, quoting Matthew Arnold,
and nothing to be done.
No fit theme for poetry. And I
remembered, sometime or other in school,
reading that. About *Empedocles*
on Etna—and then, I think, in Yeats,
who quoted it excluding Wilfred Owen from
his *Oxford Book of Modern Verse.*
You looked at me, hoping I would
understand, and yet I hadn't. . . . Because
you meant your *own* poems, those
you write and show to no one, those
that lie down darkly in some bottom drawer—
those, you thought, that did no more
than imitate a passive suffering.
I should have known.

But then what's passive
when a man of eighty-five, survivor
of two cancers, sits up all night long
to face his demons in the way he always has
and sees at dawn the black rectangle
on his disk he's made of darkness
hurled at eternity in words?
This is something to be done,
endured to be everything, fit theme
for any poem. Poems in the mind,
poems in the bottom drawer,
poems heading out past Jupiter like
mental probes launched at some far sun.
They're all the same.

You wouldn't choose
to write these poems but you are chosen.
That's endurance and the doing
and the fitness all in one. Where they go
and what becomes of them you'll never know.
If you kneel down before the winter hearth
to burn them, who's to say they'll not
be etched by fire on some unheard of stone
standing somewhere in an unknown city?

For Ernest Sandeen

Private Poem

To a friend who made a Festival and notes a time & place,
defends the 'public sphere'

Fair and fair enough! So *not*, therefore,
in that Shelford sitting room alone,
10 September, 1973,
but on a bus, the upper deck,
somewhere between Trumpington & Cambridge
fully six months earlier
and in a goodly company of folk!
An idea's rare enough that if we're going
to credit the right person
we'd better also credit the right time & place?
Well, they've come and gone four times,
those homing birds, to and from
the singing school and slugging match,
and now, I think, you weary
of it all,
                  demand the crystal clarities.

So it's like this—
                the black light that filters through
Seferis's *The Thrush*, through 1946,
through Ceri Richards' *Apple of Gower* & your poems
illuminates the private life alone
and not the 'public sphere'
however much we bellow out our lungs
in roaring, hybrid coliseums of fantasy. . . .
Clichés of theory!
Panels full of reborn, earnest suffragettes!
The black light's extinguished
in the white fluorescent light of meeting hall,
committee room, symposium and seminar.
Poems erased by Poetry.
Headlights on the routine, stupefying bus
burn into the crystal darkness
of a single room.

Public Poem

To the same, returning home from Belgrade
with his new book, 'The Manager'

We do not mange well! We do, however,
end our wanderings at some point
and come home. 1990
is as good a year as most;
and better, I suppose, counted out in pounds
than counted out in dinars.
But how fitting that the English now must
read your book on Thatcher's Britain
in Cyrillic! (You bring it home
with new wife and
new child.) Deciphering your codes,
grinning at your misdemeanors,
who prepared their case and sent you
into exile?

I take it back—
            the white light that shines
from your new book, from 1989,
from wagers with the future that would wive
and father children
surely must illuminate the city & the street
however much we bitch in our bewilderment
and, alone in single rooms, disguise
the passing of our hour as black hermetic strength
and pull down all the blinds.
In Belgrade, Miljkovi ć once wrote: *While*
you are singing, who will carry
your burden? But while you carry
your burden, who will sing your song?
Those deciphering your codes,
grinning at your misdemeanors, those
who made their case & sent you
into exile.

E.P. in Crawfordsville

for D.D. in South Bend lecturing on
"Enlightenment and Christian Dissent"

He was *en provence* for sure
at Wabash College—
Writing there to Mary Moore
of Trenton, "Grey eyes . . . "

Writing *Cino:* "Bah! I have
sung women in three
cities . . . ," putting up an
unemployed actress,

getting fired, *Gay Cino*
of quick laughter,
Cino, of the dare, the jibe.
What, asked Possum more

than once, does Ezra Pound
believe? In light. In
light from the beginning,
in gardens of the sun—

But "Pollo Phoibee, old
tin pan," in Crawfordsville?
Age de lumières! Bold
Polnesi, Jefferson, Voltaire—

light inside the acorn-seed
on Zeus's aegis-day
when he'd become indeed
the lack-land Cino

having sung & sung the sun
for thirty years in
every kind of city, light
converging into one

great ball of crystal
silent as some Hoosier
Presbyterian at prayer
along the Wabash.

F.M.F. from Olivet

(remembering Joseph Brewer)

Hueffer's Trade Route
didn't really pass
through Olivet, but Ford
had written anyway

to Italy: *Dear Bertran
de Struwwelpeter
y Bergerac*—remembering
the other's *Deah*

*ole Freiherr von
Bluggerwitzkoff, lately
Baron of the Sunken
Ports, etcetera*—

explaining that
a Small Producer might,
just there in Olivet, though
it was not Provence,

produce: "If it's good
enough for me it's
good enough for you,
concealed son o'

the authoress of *John
Halifax Gentleman*
though you be." His cor-
respondent queried him

re Distribution: of ideas,
of light, through a
Trade Route called
a Lino or a Monotype. . . .

For investment, there
was no return: Bertran of
Rapallo from Cathay
to Bluggerwitzkoff, ripe

as Memphis cotton picked
and sorted to a pip &
woven into double-breasted
stripes in Michigan:

"Does Olivet USE my text
books? Will the clog-
dancer ANSWER a few civil
questions? Let me put

it in another form: I
do not want YOUR job,
I do not want the
JOB that you have got."

Mr. Rothenstein's Rudiments

It's strange. I told that pretty girl yesterday
that yes, I knew her mother, but I knew her
great-grandmother too—Lady Burne-Jones.
It's even stranger, thinking on it, that I met
Rossetti's brother as a child; I can see
him clearly lying on that couch I rescued
for the Tate—the one on which the poet's friends
placed Shelley's body when they took it from the sea—
when I heard the house, Rossetti's, took a hit
during the blitz.
                    My father knew them all, of course—
Sir William! Whistler and Degas, Rodin, Pater,
Swinburne, Henry James. After the Slade he went
to Paris and he might have stayed,
except that Basil Blackwood, then at Balliol,
commissioned him to make that portrait drawing
that initiated the entire Oxford series
published by John Lane. So home he came and
grew more earnest reading Tolstoy, speaking
much of Probity. A French Benedictine,
and later also Eric Gill, thought
he should enter an order, or anyway go paint
at Ditchling Common. He stayed in London, though,
and met Augustus John and all the younger men.
As the influence of Whistler waned, his line began
to grow a little thick, his canvasses
just a little cluttered.

Augustus John. And Gwen. Do you realize
we nearly had Gwen John in Bronze on the embankment?
Every time I stand before the *Burghers of Calais*
I see poor Gwen. She posed for Rodin when he did
the plaster for a Whistler monument, holding

a medallion of her teacher. But because it lacked an arm—
I'd guess that half his figures lack an arm or leg—
the jury opted for a casting of the *Burghers* and
Augustus found his sister, after she had died, leaning
back against a wall in some obscure dark corner
of a Paris shed. I mean of course he found
the *plaster* of his sister . . .

     . . . Anyone who'd say that Stanley Spencer
is inferior to Arp or Mondrian can't see!
Everybody followed Fry and then got stuck somehow
on all those formal theories and by what
you'd have to call an orthodoxy after being bowled away
by Post-Impressionism. Give me Stanley Spencer
to a watered-down Matisse by Duncan Grant.
Besides, his character's of interest.
And the more we know about him and the world
he inhabited the more we see in what he made.
I'd say that's true of any artist. Also we can sometimes
understand the way a man can fill his art with
all the qualities and virtues that his life most lacks—
And that's a knowledge I prefer to Mr. Fry's
aesthetics and to all the revolutions of a Herbert Read.

Stanley! He came one night to dinner, missed
his train to Cookham, and then stayed on
for something like three months. He'd talk all day,
all night: Cookham and his painting.
His father read the bible to the children every night
and every morning Stanley walked through Cookham
seeing all the stories re-enacted in his village
by the Thames. In a way, he really did believe
they had occurred there—Jerusalem,

The emanation of his Cookham youth!
Look at his *Nativity*, his *Zacharias and Elizabeth*.
When I acquired the *Resurrection* for the Tate,
half of London sneered, half the critics
simply thought him crazy. Then they condescended,
calling him "a village pre-Raphaelite"—Spencer,
whose *Zacharias* I'd be willing to compare
even with Giotto . . .

       He did travel a bit after the war—
as far as China once. When Chou En-Lai remarked
he hoped these English now would know New China,
Stanley said he hoped New China might one day
know Cookham. . . .

        Wyndham Lewis
didn't come from Cookham—
much more likely Mars. He arrived in London
like some trigger-happy extraterritorial
and took on everything and everyone in sight.
He was, he'll probably remain, a mystery.
I knew him pretty well. And yet he'd be so
secretive he wouldn't even let you know he had
a wife after he'd been married several years.
She'd make the dinner for her husband and a guest,
set the table, then just disappear . . .

Of course it was the Fry affair, the mess
at the Omega, that was much responsible
for Lewis's mistreatment by the crowd
that wanted to control a nation's taste.
He claimed that Fry had stolen his commission
to design a sitting-room for the *Daily Mail's*
model home exhibit, then in compensation offered
him an overmantel where he'd be allowed

to execute a carving. So Lewis sent that letter
to the press about a *timid but voracious*
journalistic monster that finished him with
Bloomsbury and Fry. But in an age of log-rolling,
as he said himself, Mr. Lewis
never once was rolled . . .

                  Do you realize
that no one ever had convincingly portrayed
an ordinary business suit before the Lewis *Eliot?*
I mean with full verisimilitude, without
somehow ennobling it. There sits the poet—
in the suit he'd worn at Lloyds!

The editor of *Blast* and the friend of Ezra Pound
went to war in the artillery, then came home
and painted *Bagdad, Barcelona, Stations of the Dead.*
He said his geometrics wanted filling
and he filled them with inventions, not
with the matter of the continental Cubists.
I heard him say of Braque that one might very well
be musical or vegetarian, but life was more
than mandolins and apples.

                      And more (or maybe less!)
than all those decorations on the walls
at Charleston as well, that strange domestic
Sistine Chapel down in Sussex. I thought I'd better
go there and make my peace with Mrs. Bell
when I decided I should write on Duncan Grant.
It was not a happy visit.
I guess I said that it was my opinion
Titian couldn't draw. Anyway, she glared at me

as if I'd shot the gun that killed her son in Spain.
I've tried to do an honest job on Grant—
mainly as a decorator and the artist
of the Holland portrait and the two of Mrs. Bell.
Still, it's difficult to make ambitious claims for him
like those put forward by his friends—

and also difficult, sitting there at Charleston,
the light pouring on a garden full of flowers and
through a window on the decorated walls, the pottery,
the accumulations of a privileged life, not to think
about a painter like Gwen John, isolated and unknown,
or of my father as his reputation steadily declined
and he sat alone on the terrace at Far Oakbridge
gazing at the contours of the valley in his illness,
looking through the beauty of this world
at something he could almost see behind it.

(Cento: Passages & paraphrase from John Rothenstein's *Modern
English Painters.* Variation, derivation, & apocrypha)

Footnote on a Gift

for Laura

My friend, your teacher, gives you Rilke's *Elegies,*
reminding you that Rilke lived in Prague
when he was young. You are off to Prague
and you are young, but not as young as Rilke was
when he abandoned what he later called
a city of subordinate existences where, perhaps,
the danger was you might wake up one sunny morning
to discover you had turned into a cockroach.
But you, Laura, are already learning Czech
and do not fear in Deutsch to find subordinate
the things of new Bohemia. May everybody thrive there!
And may you thrive there with them,
teaching English which, I hope, will help them read
computer manuals & scientific articles but not,
like German once, create a separate class of citizens.
If you are not as visionary as Rainer Maria
then you are, at least, more sane. The last thing
in the world I could imagine is that you,
with all your sensible charm, would ever want
to hug an Angel rather than a human being.
You're also saner than your crazy father
who has had a dreadful year, and whose scribblings
these days sputter & meander foolishly.
He'd better, therefore, keep this short
and just say that he'll miss you.
And if you do see Angels hover over Prague,
stand still and wait. They'll fly away.
You need not whisper to the city or yourself
a misconceived intransitive—*subordinate.*

Horace Augustus Mandelstam Stalin

A poem for The Leader, either way,
but Horace found it easier.
The widow of the Russian heard for weeks
an *Os* an *Os* an *Os*—
repeating syllable of Stalin's Ode
metamorphosed as a wasp
in the iron air of Voronezh.

Imagine Mandelstam a gentle and
official poet patronized by a patrician
like Maecenas and a friend of Caesar's.
"Octavian," he'd say.
Or: "Joseph Vissarionovich."
The syllables that trail along the poems
begotten by the Stalin Ode he tried
to write say *Os*
Os, Os . . .

       wasp, axle, exile.

Others found it easier.
When their tongues were cut out, wrote
Nadezhda in her book, *still*
they praised him with their wagging stubs.

Into Cyrillic

I see they've written ПРИЈАТЕЉЪСТВО,
but it's Greek to me. They sign
it with my name. Something's been
translated, something here is very strange.

They've written ЦОН and МЕТАЈАС
and they say it isn't Greek, they say
it isn't Russian either and I see
my name. I point to Macedonia,

to Leningrad. But everything, they
tell me, points to Kosovo. Everything
they tell me points to Sarajevo too.
For example, ПРИЈАТЕЉЪСТВО.

I ask them, did I write that word?
They found it in my poem. They say I stood
with Miloš Obilić in 1389: everybody
heard me shouting LAZARUS!

I tell them I was silent; if there, I stood
aside. They say I stood among
the Yugovići as in 1989 I stood between
Milosović and Karadžić.

I'm tangled in Cyrillic and I cannot
find my way. They'll help me.
They'll lead me on. I say I want to be
led out of this, away.

They say ПРИЈАТЕЉСТВО!
The trains have all stopped running and
there is no petrol for the cars.
Everyone is shouting ЦОН, ЦОН, ЦОН!

Bogomil in Languedoc

One stone at Domazan is enough.
In southern France among
the Catharist sarcophagi beyond
a village full of tiled roofs.

He is the warrior of Radimlja and he
has come this far. He raises both his arms.
He spreads wide both enormous hands.
Although he is entirely silent here,

his mason, up from Tuscany and
proselytizing slogs along the hot Apennine,
spouted bits he'd learned from
Interrogatio Johannis to his missionary

friend who left the book at Carcassonne.
When all matter is to be destroyed,
the stone warrior here at Domazan
will give the sign. He will finally

drop his arms. And where he stood
the hole in space will spread until
all nothing speaks in tongues to no one.
May he, then, forever raise his hands.

The Singer of Tales

for Charles Simic

I

It's a strange sound
the first time you hear it

it's a kind of moan
& the old man bows in his lap

on the one taut string
of his *gusle*

warming up as if he were a kind of
West Virginian or a

Smoky Mountain fiddler
but the blues he has to play

the sorrow he will tell goes back
six hundred years

then it was almost too much to bear
but now he sings

II

Nothing of it written down
before the 1600s

They fled from Maritsa from Kosovo
the final loss at Smederevo

and settled where they could
around Regusa in the islands

on the Adriatic coast or Herzegovina
in Bosnia the Montenegrin hills

No one saw quite what had happened yet
No one sang about it

    III

Then somebody did
Sang until his song recalled

the blackbirds from the field the bones
from shallow graves the banners

from oblivion the ichor bleeding from
the wounded ikon in the monastery's corner room

Sang until his voice failed utterly to sing
and then he moaned

and then he whispered weeping
in the whispering dark air

Now it is almost too much to bear
but then he sang

The Silence of Stones

I

In Bosnia, in Herzegovina nearby: enigmatic
standing stones proclaim
some mode of life that lost its way

upon the very field of light
where men and women danced the *kolo* once
and called to vine and lily,

wheeling sun and sickle moon, sheep and deer
and falcon: brother, sister.
Where the waters of Radimlja dry in dusty summer

enormous hands on the sarcophagi
spread their fingers wide in greeting or in admonition.
Hieratic, fetishistic.

Long before Lord Tvrtko left for Kosovo.

II

Some mode of life. Some field of light.
Before the list of Manichaean crimes
Drawn up by Torquemada for the Pope in Rome,

The Pope in Avignon was heard to whisper
Dobri Bosniani to his agents
up from Languedoc, reminding them of speech that

crawleth like a crab & heretics who *creepeth in humility*
upon St. Catherine's Eve when conflagration
would consume the hills and plains, the rocks and trees,

falcons, sheep, and wild deer
of that far place already near brought down before
Lord Tvrtko left for Kosovo

Where raised hands admonish or salute.

   III

Admonish or salute. Some mode of life,
some field of light whereon they dance the *kolo*
holding hands, where feet tread gently

in the dust beside the dry and stony bed of the Radimlja.
On stećak, mramor, upright slab or obelisk,
40,000 hands rise up in solemn gesture of some last

refusal or compliance, join together then
beneath the wheeling sun, the sickle moon, there among
the animals and calligraphic ornament,

vine & lily, brother falcon, sister lamb or fawn,
Dobri Bosniani spoken for
in Avignon but silent on this silent plain

Long before and after Tvrtko left for Kosovo.

A Wind in Roussillon

I

The Tramontane that's blowing pages
of an unbound book through Roussillon
departs on schedules
of its own. . . .

Et nous, les os . . . et nous, les os.
And us, the bones.

II

The train departs from Austerlitz on time.
After Carcassonne, Tuchan,
wheat and barley dry up in the sun
& trees appear hung heavily
with cherries, lemons, oranges.

Red tiled roofs are angled oddly
on the little houses in the hills below Cerdagne.
Gray slate's left behind.

By the tracks
a villager has nailed up a goat's foot
and a sunflower to the door
that opens on his vineyard
circled by a wall of heavy stones.

III

In French, the words of Mme T. about les îles Malouines sound
nearly as bizarre as ads for the religious kitsch at Lourdes trans-
lated into English in the same edition of *Le Monde* . . . "A see-
through plastic model of the Virgin with unscrewable gold crown
enables you to fill the image up with holy water from a tap." And
Mme T., *qui a félicitée les forces armées,* swells in French to the dimen-
sions of a Bonaparte: *le plus merveilleuses du monde* . . . *le courage et
l'habileté ont donné une nouvelle fierté à ce pays et nous ont fait compren-
dre que nous étions vraiment une seule famille.*

Et nous, les os: vraiment une seule famille.

IV

Low hills dense with yellow broom!
Cactus, thistles, wild mountain roses;
lavender and holly and convolvulus.
Above the rows of plane trees,
olive groves root down through rock.
Above the olive groves, cypresses & pines.

Down the valley under Canigou
a helicopter dips and passes overhead,
circles the Clinique Saint-Pierre
whining like a homing wasp.
Landing in an asphalt parking lot,
it scatters old men playing skittles, boules.
Young men wearing orange flight suits
carry something human
wrapped in white inside.

V

The name of one low, ruined house
in Perpignan is John
and Jeanne. (It's in another country.)
When great winds pass the threshold
nothing sings or appears.

It's John & Jeanne
and from their graying faces
falls the plaster of day. (Far off
the most ancient one,
the arch daughter of shadows.)

You build a fire in the cold great hall
and you withdraw.
(Your name is Yves Bonnefoy.)
You build it there, and you withdraw.

VI

My hostess came to Perpignan from Dublin more than forty years
ago. Now in her late sixties, she lives in the third floor flat of an
elegant eighteenth-century house in what were once the servants'
quarters. The walls are full of books on Cathar heresies and
Albigensians and Templars. When the south of France was flayed
for twenty years in the Crusades, blood ran all the way from
Montségur to the Queribus Château before it finally dried. Mme
Danjou came here with the Quakers when the Spanish Civil War
broke out and helped Republican refugees across the border at Port
Bou. Four years later she was helping Jews across the border in the
opposite direction when the Roussillon was occupied by the Nazis.
Denounced by a neighbor, she was thrown in jail where she waited

for the train that would take her to a prison camp in Germany. Like
other European women of her generation, she is tough. "One felt,"
she says, struggling for a moment with the English that she rarely
speaks these days, "that one had work to do." The war had ended
by the time the Nazis sent the train.

VII

Not only the delimited circumferences
but also all the white stone houses
in the streets of southern Catholic cemeteries
speak of walled towns by Vauban
or by his foretypes in the Middle Ages or before.
This silent town within the town of Collioure
where Derain and Picasso paid their bills
with paintings no one wanted yet
fortifies itself against the naked bathers
and the tourists at the Templiers.
I intrude upon the silent tenants searching
for Antonio Machado.

The wealthy dead inhabit their expensive homes
and wait impatiently for quick descendants
to arrive and fill each empty room marked *reservée*.
The poor lie down in dresser drawers stacked high
in marble walls around a central Calvary
and whisper without any *nouvelle fierté à ce pays*:
"Nous étions vraiment une seule famille."

Machado fled from Franco's armies
first to Barcelona, then across the border
with some refugees. Dying, he came

on foot, and in the rain, and with his mother.
He left the room they gave him only once
to walk alone along the streets of Collioure
before they brought him here.
He sings these dead his mortal words forever.
Globo del fuego ... disco morado ...

The sun that parched the bones
dries up the town, dries up the southern sea.
Savilla is distant and alone.
Sol. Soleil.
Castile, and Collioure! Machado.

VIII

With knife or nail or glass someone clumsily
has scratched into the blackened wooden gate
that's chained high up beyond one's reach
at Fort Saint-Elme: *Privée, Bien Gardée.*

A small green lizard darts between two stones.
It looks to be deserted in the tower, and yet
it's difficult to tell. Everything inside
has been restored. They say it's lived in now.

Climbing here, I heard two cuckoos answering
each other down the valley. A kestrel hovers high
and drops to earth the far side of the tower.
No sound now but northern wind on fortified étoile.

The level sea below me mirrors Le Château Royal
that Dugommier won back for revolution after
Dufour's treason turned the cannon of Saint-Elme
on quiet Collioure for money and for Spain.

From the col de Banyuls through Port-Vendres
they'd advanced. Then, bien gardée, Saint-Elme.
A captain stood about where I stand, bargaining.
Dufour let him quickly through the gates.

No one sang the cruel cannonade they loosed
on the Château which burned away the Middle Age
from rampart, hall and tower. Dugommier won back
the smoking bones before which once some

pitiful last troubadour sang out to Templars
gazing down at him beside the sea. No one gazes
down from Fort Saint-Elme. Nor do I sing out
Dòna, maries de caritat . . .
                                        Lady, mother of charity . . .
I was born too late. . . .

IX

Tour de la Massane, Tour de Madeloc. Towers like these stretch
along the backbone of the Pyrenees and look down on the plain
of Roussillon, the southern coast, and Spain. By day the little
garrisons would signal to each other with a puff of smoke, by night
with fire. Valerius Flaccus, Commandant at Madeloc, left his chis-
elled mark on the great rock. In Rome, they put him on a coin. In
Roussillon, les os. *Que malvaise chançon de nos chanté ne seit,* he might

have said a little later and little to the west. What he said, in fact, was this:

VALERIUS FLACCUS
PRAEFECTUS PRAESIDII MONUMENTUM JUSSIT
VIVUS SIBI CONDI LOCO
INTERCEPTO ET EMUNITO

The buried temple spits no mud or rubies out. The sun pours down upon the tower that now relays the television news from Paris, London, Rome, and even as far off as Las Malvinas or The Lebanon. I sit in my hotel and drink in martial music from the streets of Buenos Aires. Then we see Israeli tanks annihilate Beirut. Communication is a subtle thing through our electric sepulchre. In the Punic wars, Valerius could only talk in hyperbolic terms with smoke and fire. . . . Power hymns instalments to its spirit now in all works of impatience: wars, towers, rituals, TV. In memory, Valerius, you arise. Like an occult language found in an iron-bound book.

X

Mother of charity, Mother of consolation,
Your house is not La Tour Madeloc,
Mother of bones, Mother of dissolution.

Lady of leisure, Lady of Roussillon,
Maître Xinxet has blackened your hermitage,
Lady of landfall, Lady of languors.

Mother of ostentation, Mother of ordure,
Neptune rests in your chapel,
Mother of noon, Mother of nightshade.

Lady of purdah, Lady of purchase,
The village cries out for rain,
Lady of drought, Lady of departures.

Mother of Jesus, Mother of jackals,
The pilgrim is flaying the Jew,
Mother of olives, Mother of obeisance,

Lady binding the book in leather & iron,
Mother of scattered pages,
Work of secret patience, Tramontane.

Northern Summer

The flight of sentimentality through empty space.
Through its elliptical hole
an heraldic blackbird's
black wings, yellow beak, round eyes, with the yellow
ring, which defines its inner empty
space

— GÖRAN SONNEVI

I THE CASTLE

                    Occupies
a picturesque
commanding strong position
on the summit of a cliff some forty
feet in height
the base of which is covered
up at flood tide by the waters of the Forth.
Large, magnificent, commodious
with rock nearby and wood and water to afford
the eye a picture of a rare
and charming beauty
forming a delightful and romantic spot
the sight of which
could not but amply compensate et
cetera
                    the language of a tour book
threading aimlessly
through sentimental empty space.

Or build on, say, an Edward's language
to his dear and faithful cousin
Eymar de Valance
like a second generation builds upon

the ruins of a first?

                finding not
in our
Sir Michael Wemyss
good word
nor yet good service and
that he now shows himself in such a wise
that we must hold him traitor
and our enemy we do command you that ye
cause his manor where we lay
and all his other manors to be burned his lands
and goods to be destroyed
his gardens to be stripped all bare
that nothing may remain
and all
may thus take warning—

Language
moving upon consequence
Consequence
upon a language: Flight
of an heraldic bird
through space that is inhabited.

Some say Bruce had raised his standard here.

II PIED-À-TERRE

I live between the castle and the coal mine
in a folly. It's the truth.
They put a roof on it last year. I have
a room, a window on the sea.

            Strange to say, I
haven't seen my host yet,
Captain Wemyss.
He's holed up in his castle in this awful rain.
I'm holed up in my folly
with my pads and pens.
If the sun comes out this month, maybe yet
we'll meet
a-walking in the garden O.

            "Baron Wemyss of Wemyss"
all the old books call
his many forbears.
Do I just shout out *hello there*
Wemyss of Wemyss?
Seven centuries of purest Scottish pedigrees,
says Mr. F., the Edinburgh historian.
Twenty-seven generations.
I can offer
just one eighth of watery Kirkpatrick.

The flight of sentimentality through empty space!
A rhetoric, at least; (an awkward line).
The flight of Sentiment
is through a space that's occupied.

This space is occupied, all right,
and I am guest
of both the present and the past.

    The past
begins in caves,
the Gaelic *Uamh* soon enough becoming Wemyss.
James the Fifth surprised
a band of gipsies in one cave, drinking there
and making merry. Though he
could join them incognito in his famous role
as Godeman of Ballangeich
and share their mad hilarity, James the Sixth
would only shout out *treason*
when he panicked of a sudden, claustrophobic,
in a *Uamh* become a mine.

Above the caves and mines they built this house.

And put a chaplain in it! I find there was
no piper here, and worse, no bard—
But Andrew Wyntoun, a prior of St Serf,
wrote a family chronicle in verse
& praised
    An honest knycht
and of good fame
Schir Jhone of Wemyss by his rycht name.

Well, if I'm the guest of absent hosts
the cost of lodging here a while
is neither waived
nor anywhere within my calculation—
(the flight of Sentiment

is not
through empty space) .

Did Mynyddog Mynfawr, camped along the Forth,
feed the brave Gododdin mead and wine
a year
a year
a year?

Or did he send them sober down his mine?

III THE MINE

The flight through empty space of Sentiment
—mentality! There's nothing
sentimental
within sight of this abandoned mine.
From where I stand
I'd talk about dead gods, I think.
                        From where I stand on this
deserted beach
between the castle and the mine
I think I'd say the legates
of the dead god Coal
had built his image here to look
exactly like a gallows made of iron & alloy
high enough
to hang a giant from—

The tower's erect upon the hill, but nothing moves.

Who worked here once?
No Free Miners from the Forest of Dean
have hewn the coalface down the ages
here at Wemyss from when
the coughing grey-eyed servants
won the coal
for monks at prayer in freezing Dunfermline
but virtual slaves. No *gales*, no lease
for them.
            "Coal beneath the soil
shall be inherited with soil
and property." The lairds of Fife could pack
a Privy Council and by act of law
reduce a man to serfdom. He
was bought or sold
along with his equipment. His child
went underground at six
to earn an extra seven pence
lest he sail to Noroway with Sir Patrick Spence.

The tower's erect upon the hill, and nothing moves.

When the fire leapt down the tunnel, forked and dove,
an age had come and gone. The
nation voted Labour
but the coal board blundered here in Wemyss
at once.
            The lift plunged down
through all that soaring iron and alloy, down
to where the caves and tunnels
smoulder uselessly and spread the fire
on inland through
bituminous rich veins. It could burn

a hundred years. It could burn as far as London.

Miles of heavy cable lie around me
on the beach. Almost ankle-thick, it unravels
like a length of rope left over
from a hanging. It raised and lowered the lift.
The lift descended with amazing speed.
With amazing speed
the fire leapt down the tunnel, forked and dove.
Everyone, I think, got out.

A tanker steams across the bleak horizon.

The tower's erect upon the hill.

IV A QUEEN

John Knox said the visit of the Queen
had raised the price
of wild fowl sufficiently
that partridges were sold at half a crown.
He was not a sentimental man.
Of the Regent's coronation
he'd remarked: "Seemly
as to put a saddle on the back
of an unruly cow."
                    O belle
et plus que belle crooned
Mary's friend, Ronsard. Better him than Knox
for gentle conversation?
Better all the Medicis & better maybe
little sick king Frank

whose inflammation of the middle ear
and abscess of the brain
were dear to Calvin.
                And yet her keen eyes
danced out of a window here
in February, 1565.
It was cold that year in Fife.
Every fireplace here at Wemyss was blazing
full of fine Wemyss coal
when Mary gazed at Charles Darnley riding by.
Yesterday was warm & bright
when Peggy, who's the cook, pointed
out the window, showing me
where Darnley had dismounted. I had come
to get a pan to heat some water in.
He had come to woo a queen,
win the Matrimonial Crown and full equality
of Royal right, make every kind
of mischief in the realm. The empty space
between the window and
the place he stood beside his horse
in sexy tight black hose was filled at once
with Feeling—

Darnley sang a song more serious than Ronsard's
and Bothwell entered in his
little book that Kirk o'Field's convalescent
suffered from *roinole* and not
petite verole—
                syphilis, not smallpox.
But that was later on.
At Wemyss it was a sentimental morning.

V A PRINCE

Or talk about Charles Edward then.
Charles, Edward, Louis,
Sylvester, Maria, Casimir, Stewart.
The Bonnie Prince himself,
the grand Chevalier. To the Forty-Five
this castle sent Lord Elcho.
Kindred of my own kin's forbears, my
brooding and attainted
absent host,
              he gazed from Holyrood
through gilded ballrooms & out casement windows
at the gillies & the pipers & the clans
weighing odds, meditating
languages—Gaelic, French, the
lisped Italian English of the Regent Prince.

      The King enjoy his ain again?
Doubtful, but for honour
one must risk in any case this autumn theatre
although it issue
in a winter's desolation. . . .

Claymore!—
           (or is it *Gardyloo?*)—echoes
even now from Holyrood
through Fife. Beneath those Strathspey
dancers' feet when Elcho's mother
led off celebrations
of the rout at Prestonpans,
history smouldered with surprises

older than the coal fields
on the Wemyss estate.
Language moved upon inconsequence
and consequence
at once: *Will you see me
to my quarters?* and

No quarter . . .

as if you'd hear two voices whispering
behind you while you stared
down Royal Mile thinking of the sheltered hollow
under Arthur's seat. . . .

The empty space between the window
framing Elcho and the place the clansmen camped
filled up in time with sentimental tales
and the progeny
of all those partridges
whose price the visit of the Scottish Queen
had raised, said Knox, to half a crown.
And yet his line of vision then
was tangent to
the flight of an heraldic bird
whose spiral into time
was on a furious northern wind—
vehement,
and with a terrifying sound.

VI A VOICE

I hear my mother's voice reading Stevenson—
or is it Scott? Someone's wandering lost

among the heather. I must be eight or nine.
I know I should be reading this myself,
but when I read the words the voice I hear
ceases to be hers. . . .
                There is a space
I have not learned to fill
somewhere between printed marks and sounds
and I am lost in some way too
among the heather, frightened of the distances
when all I want to do is drift on lang
uage into dream. . . .
             "*Cha n'eil Beurl' agam* . . . "
someone says, but I follow him
in any case on hands & knees in terror.
Have I got the silver button in my teeth?
Am I papered for the murder of that
Campbell back in Appin? We're through
the cleft, the Heugh of Corrynakiegh,
and now the moor: it's black and burned
by heath fires. Moorfowl cry.
The deer run silently away from us. . . .

Or am I underneath the castle of my enemy?
And is my enemy my only friend? I hear
the sentinel calling out in English
All's well, All's well
but we crawl off toward a hovel
made of stone & turf & thatch. There's
a fire inside, and over it a small iron pot.
The ancient crone who's stirring it
offers me a boiled hand
                to steal away
some gentleman's attention

from his Ovid . . . and pack him off to bed
with images to mingle
with his dreams, said R.L.S. to Baxter.
And Scott: that "laws & manners
cast a necessary colouring;
but the bearings, to use heraldic language,
will remain the same,
though the tincture may be different
or opposed. . . . "
                    Bearings . . . tincture . . .
Theft and Dream,
flight of an heraldic bird through language,
and my mother's voice.

Who are the Kirkpatricks? where is Abbotsford?
How can poor sick R.L.S., listening with
his Hoosier wife, hear off in Samoa "beaten bells"
from just across the Firth?

For a moment, laws and manners seem no
more than colouring. Charles Edward back in Paris
casts a medal of himself—*Carolus Walliae*
Princeps—and the future hangs
on messages delivered by the likes of
Alan Breck from men like Cluny
in his cage—
language moving upon consequence. . . .

          But time has gone to live with
Waverleys and Balfours, with townies
like Rankeillor and his lowland lawyer ilk.
I am awake in Fife. I hear
the distant echoes of my mother's voice reading.

Sentiment's transfigured into history,
and history to sentiment.

VII KIRKCALDY

In Kirkcaldy one considers economics.
We need a dozen eggs. I leave my folly, catch
a bus near Wemyss, and walk around
this "old lang toun" that bears the name
of Mary's last defender.
Loyal old Kirkcaldy, last
support and stay of an unlucky queen,
scourge of Bothwell, keeper
of the craggy rock in Edinburgh
out of which your one-time friend John Knox
would pry you even with his
final fetid breath—
                                    Linoleum?
In June
descendents of those Covenanters Cromwell shot
treat their jute with linseed oil
where William Adam, stone & lime Vanbrughian,
built in Gladney House
a Netherlandish lesson for his sons
and Adam Smith returned in early middle age
and wrote.

Did Elcho see young Robert Adam on the castle wall
where John Knox saw Kirkcaldy? each one
moving through the crystal chambers
of his mind to build more perfect measurements
before the cannon fired

of distances heraldic birds might fly,
language moving upon consequence
to say *Nobility,*
Salvation, Space?
          When Adam left
Kirkcaldy grammar school
for Edinburgh, Smith enrolled at
Glasgow, never mentioning (when he
returned at forty-five) the Forty-Five.
"The workmen carry nails instead
of money to the baker's shop and alehouse.
The seat of empire should remove itself
to that part of the whole
contributing the greatest share to its support.
In sea-port towns a little grocer
can make forty-five percent upon a stock. Capitals
increased by parsimony
are diminished by misconduct, prodigality.... "
And not a word about the bonded miners
in the collieries & salt pits.

Economies! Those workmen died
in nailers' dargs to earn a casual footnote.
That parsimony made a bigot certain he was saved,
his neighbour rightly damned.
That seat of empire never moved;
its rebel colonies themselves became imperious.
Those country houses made by Adam and his sons
rose up with fortresses
they built at Inverness on orders straight
from Cumberland, which bled.

The smell of jute on linseed

stinks of deprivation: linoleum peels off floors
of little grocers in this town
where faces in the baker's shop and alehouse
thirst for darker oils
sucked up Shell, BP, and Exxon rigs
from underneath the bottom of the sea.

The Regent dragged Kirkcaldy from his rock
and hung him on the gallows Knox prepared him for:
face against the sun.
His blinded eyes beheld a crazy German
sitting firmly on a Stuart throne.
History gave William Pitt *The Wealth of Nations*,
the brothers Adam peel-towers & Fort George.

Beggared sentiment flew straight into the hills

VIII OSSIAN, ETC.

And metamorphosed there in Ossianic melancholy.
James Macpherson heard, he said,
the howling of a northern wind; he heard old men
chanting through the night about the woods
of Morven; Selma filled, he wrote,
with names & deeds—Fingal's, Oscar's, Gaul's—
but language threaded aimlessly through empty spaces
& through languorous dreams, *with rock nearby*
and wood and water to afford the eye
a rare and charming beauty, the sight of which
could not but amply compensate
admirers of the sentimental and the picturesque.
Where better read a "forgery" than in a folly?

And shall I like these poems
that David Hume defended when he found
the heroes' names authenticated
by an inventory of all the Highland mastiffs?
Napoleon did, who never heard of Dr Johnson,
but who carried *Fingal* into battle
imitating, now and then, with relish,
the Ossianic style in his memos & dispatches.
And Goethe, caught up in the turmoil
of his *Sturm und Drang,* built
the European Zeitgeist from a massive
mountain sadness caught in far Temora.
Staring at Macpherson's book,
they filled the emptiness before their eyes
with what they were.
                            It was an age
of forgeries & fakes: Pretenders
old and young, gothic ruins in the garden,
memories of casket letters, padded
coats and powdered wigs. And while Macpherson
roamed the hills in search of Gaelic bards,
a London dealer named Buchanan
sold the Earl of Wemyss a phony Venus
signed *Van Dyck:* "the sight of which could
not but amply compensate," etcetera,
Buchanan whispered softly in the noble ear,
and rubbed his hands, and grinned.
Staring at the canvas on his castle wall,
the Earl filled the emptiness before his eyes
with what he thought he saw.

"The Erse Nation may be furious with Lord North,

for even Fingal tells him so,
but adds: 'And yet, my Lord, I do not
desert you." Walpole, 1782.
Macpherson travelled south & changed his style,
learning, it appears, a language moving
upon consequence, and consequently moved among
the circles of the powerful & into spaces
occupied by EICs and Nabobs. With a pamphlet
written for Mohamed Ali Chan, he scattered
all the nouveaux riches in London.

               To my surprise,
I find I rather like him,
this child of the Macpherson clan
who came to be MP from Camelford and drive
a private coach, though it's true
I cannot read his book for very long.
Who can say what spoke to him
in Ruthven, tiny village on the Highland Road
near Perth where plowmen unearthed shards
of Roman bowls & where the farmers
scratched St Kattan's name as *Chattan*
on the Druid stones. Here he saw
an end that emptied the entire north
of ancient feeling. The broken clansmen
staggered to his very door. It was
the Highland Army's last assembly; Cluny had
a price upon his head; Macphersons fled,
then hid him; Charles was somewhere
in the islands or in France. The barracks
where Macpherson played a soldier burned,
and he was nine. Then enormous quiet.

I close the book and walk out on the shingle
staring into low wet fog upon the Firth
that rolls against the rocks like spindrift.
The beach is empty, save for one old man
and one black bird that's flying toward the mine.
The limbs of trees are heavy, drip—
as if with melting snow.

                    When old men faltered
in their songs
Macpherson squared the widening empty circles
with what came to hand: with rocks,
with fogs, with dripping trees, deserted beaches
and old men by which heraldic birds
were briefly lured to perch
on names like *Fingal, Oscar, Gaul*
as if on severed limbs upon a field of slaughter
the sight of which did not appal
the rock nearby or wood and water which afforded
the clear eye a rare and charming beauty
where the Erse Nation was not furious with Lord North.
Seeking to fill emptiness, Macpherson
marked its boundaries,
surveyed & gerrymandered sentimental space—

Samuel Johnson filled that space
with rage, Napoleon with a military will.
They too longed for grander feelings; an actual object
and a cause. Heraldic birds appeared
on the horizon, flying north.
Macpherson travelled south.
The Earl of Wemyss stared happily upon his Venus
signed *Van Dyck.*

IX

And I stare quizzically at what I've written here,
at language that has used me one more time
for consequential or inconsequential ends that
are not mine. Can I tell which (& where)
by making declarations: the one? the other, now?
By speaking Edward's language
to his dear and faithful cousin, Eymar de Valance,
as a second generation speaks
the ruins of a first?
                            by finding not
in our
Sir Michael Wemyss
good word? or occupying picturesque positions
on the summit of a cliff?

Can I tell which (& whose) by calling points
that mark the intersection of some arbitrary boundaries
castle, queen, and *mine?*
boundaries of a space by no means empty
where the cost of lodging
is exacted by a pile of books, by *castle, queen,* and *mine,*
attainted absent lord, and black heraldic bird?
I close the book and walk out on the shingle
starting into low wet fog, etcetera.
I never closed the book. I never left the room
to walk along the beach.

                     Tourist? Paying guest—
of language of
the place, but heading further north

and pledging silence.
I've heard a scholar filled his empty life
by tracing down a thousand plagiaries from eighty
sources in MacP. I've heard the casket letters
occupied a thousand scholars who had emptiness to fill
for half a thousand years. Otherwise,
who knows, they might have filled those spaces
with the motions of a Bothwell or a Cumberland
through whom the language of the place
spoke itself to consequence.

I've heard a man found Waverley "so colourless
and unconvincing as to be
a virtual
                    gap on the page."

And where are you, Kirkpatrick?   (& Matthias)

Or you—
          whose little ship ran battle-scarred
before the wind to Norway, piloted
by Hanseatic sailors well past lowland Karmoi.
Did you follow then the rocky coast to Bergen?
and from there a black heraldic bird
to Copenhagen, Malmö? Did you sail north from Orkney
shouting into gales, spoken for by oaths,
language howling you to silence deep as Dragsholm?
Did she say, whose French was not
Brantôme's, whose verse appalled Ronsard,
l'oiseau sortira de sa cage? And did she say, before
Kirkcaldy chased you through the mists
around the Orkneys, *Sonnets in italic hand*
conjure you to Scania. . . .

You'll crawl in squalid circles for eleven years & more
widdershins
and widdershins, weeping. . . .

So Bothwell's route is mine. I'll stuff my mouth
with herring, think of Anna Throndsen,
and not return to Fife either with the Maid of Norway
or the Duke of Orkney's head.
My bird of Sentiment took flight from Inverness.
Tangent to our Baltic steamer's course, he's plighted
to a Hanseatic taxidermist who will stuff him
for an øre —
              Or: *l'oiseau sortira de sa cage?*

Old Bert Brecht, wily exile,
fleeing just ahead
of the Gestapo,
making for L.A. by way of Finland,
did you really see "High up in Lapland
towards the polar arctic sea,
a smallish hidden door"?

Through that door *black wings, yellow beak*
round eyes . . .

                    appear a moment, pause

                    & disappear

Part V

While You Are Singing

While you are singing
who will carry your burden?
While you alone defy
the poverty of clarity?

While you encounter bitter fruit
and the sarcastic dew
while you are singing
who will carry your burden?

Travel. Sing. Defy.
Only the poem desires you
and the night reveres you.
But while you are singing

Who will carry your burden?

Translated with Vladeta Vucković
from the Serbian of Branko Miljković

'Void which falls out of void . . . '

a

Void which falls out of void, transparent,
cones, hemispheres,
fall through empty space.
Thoughtform, crescent, trajectory.

b

However relevant!
In the infinite freedom I can
keep back, give
my notes resilience, in relation
to each other, to my whole body, which also
falls in infinity through empty space:
e.g.
Charlie Parker's solo in *Night in Tunisia* on May 15th 1953.

c

The flight of sentimentality through empty space.
Through its elliptical hole
an heraldic blackbird's
black wings, yellow beak, round eyes, with the yellow
ring, which defines its inner empty
space.

translated with Göran Printz-Påhlson
from the Swedish of Göran Sonnevi

On Rereading a Friend's First Book

You are 4000 miles away &
this world did not invite us.

OBERT HASS

These poems discussed by all the critics now
as if they had been written by a poet
dead a hundred years—

How young we were!

I see my poet in parodic costume
mumming Marshal Ky
or maybe General Westmoreland
as all of us around the burning microphone
give the finger to the war
and Stanford's Hoover Institute.
Everything was art and politics and Eros.

Everything was Eros.

Why is there nostalgia for incendiary times?
Because some Helen's at
the center of the fire. That girl in the t-shirt
and the shorts who loves your voice,
who puts your words into her mouth, who
comes back to your room when all the speeches
have been made.

I knew her too. You wrote of longing
and desire as if they could undo
the malice of the times.
You burned at night like napalm.
Now those days

are like the pyracanthas in these poems,
and we like waxwings, drunk on them.

The world looks almost to have invited us.

Two in New York

I EASTER 1912

His name was Frédéric Sauser his name
was Blaise Cendrars his name was Nineteen Twelve
his name was Eiffel Tower.

Only later Sonia Delaunay and Trans-Siberian Prose,
later loss of a good right arm at the Marne.
His name that day it was Pâques might have been Ray—

Ray of Gourmont that Easter and everyone gone.
Nobody liturgy nobody nun nobody
anthem or song or prelate or incense or drum.

So *dic nobis quid vidisti:* nobody nobody there
when he woke and wrote down his name
in New York it was Fear. What could he do but go home?

II CHRISTMAS 1929

And what could *he* do, Chien Andalou,
whose speech had the fire of flamenco guitar,
whose eyes were the gypsies of war.

Federico gracias gracias (loricated legionaries
looking like a Guardia Civil before its time,
the Harlem jazzmen blowing bagels from the bells

of saxaphone and horn: *Christus natus est)*—
Feed the poor on *cante jondo,* give the weary rest.
But what could he do, Chien Andalou,

Poeta en Nueva York? Shiva looked like Ramadan.
And yet the girls were rain. He'd ransom every
singing boy he'd die for, and he'd die for it in Spain.

Easter 1912 and Christmas 1929:
Blaise Cendrars and Garcia Lorca in New York
(a second take)

What lengths what loops. In 1912 and
good enough. In 1929.
At Easter first, at Pâques. And then a good
right hand and arm blown off
the shoulder at the Battle of the Marne.
And after 1930, the Falange.
But Easter first, but Christmas next again.
A calendar, a caliper.
And One:
who'd done a juggling act with Chaplin
in the London circus once.
One: who'd hear
a violin in limousine, a xylophone in linotype.
Who'd call out *Negro Negro* to the King
of Harlem looking for the Gypsy Jesus Christ.
In 1912, in 1929.
Caruso sang Puccini & the widows in black
carried his cross through the Bronx.
Whose Red Christ or whose Black Sun split
apart like a coal? Did somebody say
Je connais . . . Je descends
à grands pas vers le bas de la ville?
Did somebody answer
with wheel and leather and hammer and oil?
Ninguno quería ser . . .
Ninguno amaba las hojas, la lengua azul.
First Cendrars in 1912. And Lorca next.
One: These three:
Chalice and orchid and book. All the Christs
all the heists in museums. Nobody
there to hear bells, nobody anthem and song,
nobody liturgy, nobody nun, nobody

prelate or drum.
So *dic nobis quid vidisti* nobody nobody
there: Encores encipher at dawn.
Ten: What tense? Who'd tell
what tensions tore the whorish times.
They're all at nines who once were six & seven.
War and crash and war once more
within the loops upon the lengths & tongs.
The Russians all wore sarafans the cats
all wore kokoshniks.
Only Andalusians barked like the dogs.
Where bankrupts dealt in a contraband Duende
how could you dwell in the Blancos del Oro
Kingdom come where nobody came?
One: who dressed himself like a bride.
One: *que se viste de novia.*
One: who came back all alone to his room
whose bed was cold as a tomb
who had heard a hundred thousand women sing,
a hundred thousand cellos:
Cent milles femmes, cent milles violoncelles.
One: These Two.
Blaise Cendrars and Chien Andalou
with flamenco guitar.
In 1912 good enough in 1929.
Before the Marne before the carnage in Spain.
At Easter first, but Christmas next again.
Chalice and orchid and book.
Length and loop, anthem and gongs,
limousine xylophone linotype library songs.

Two in Harar

I SIR RICHARD BURTON, 1854

He learned Somali from the soft and plaintive voice
of Kadima who allowed him to remove the leather lace
stitching up her labia and put two fingers in.

This was anthropology, linguistics. Toplogy and trade
would come in turn. Calling himself Haji Mirza Abdullah,
he wore a silken girdle with a dirk & chewed on khat

he found sufficiently priapic that in time he'd force his
member through infibulations of the local girls
without unlacing first. Now he rose and went to work.

He'd play the Amir off against al-Haji Sharmakay
on matters touching eunuchs and the slaves.
He'd demonstrate Koranic scholarship, say *Allahu Akhbar.*

He'd mesmerize them with his tales from the *Nights.*
His exegesis of *The Sura* dazzled all the mullahs
and he wisely took a local *abban* from among the Isas.

By the southwest coast near Zayla he turned inland,
riding on a donkey with a shotgun on his knee.
Everything that was not stone was sand. Everything that

was not sun was dust and wind. His bodyguards were
Long Gulad, The Hammal, End of Time.
They sang him Belwos, fed him holcus for his colic,

millet beer and boiled barks. If the nomads took him
he would learn phallotomy, his penis gone
for scholarship among the wives in someone's tent.

Bedu lurked about his camp and hurled stones.
They called him Old Woman, Chief of Zayla, Painted Man.
They called him Turk & Priest & Pilgrim—Merchant,

Banyan, and Calamity Sent Down from God.
He gave up his disguise and forged a letter from the
Aden consul introducing him as an ambassador

and dressed up in his captain's uniform with
epaulets and sword. He marched until he saw the walls
no white man ever breached, the gate he thought

he'd walk through chanting poems. Back in Zayla
they proclaimed him dead. Back in London
Karl Marx & Tennyson sat down to read his Mecca Haj.

The Amir asked him if he'd come to buy Harar.

II ARTHUR RIMBAUD, 1886–1888

And was Harar for Sale? And were *Le Voyant's* visions
null and void? *Solde.* He'd left behind what time
nor science had acknowledged, drowned his book of magic

and returned to earth. And one must enter splendid cities
absolutely modern after all. Among the packs
of one-eyed mangy dogs. And with a taste for soil & stone.

His I was other and another still. His ear once made
him brass and like a bugle he had blown.
A scent of wood, he'd found himself a broken violin.

He did not think he knew and did not want to know
how he'd been thought into his poems.
He colored vowels no more and all of them went black.

He'd be a gun-butt now if he were wood;
if he were steel, a rail laid down in Africa for desert trains.
He studied business, engineering, crafts.

He'd sold unknown harmonic intervals for
proper calculation and would traffic
in the hides and coffee-beans and ivories of Somalia

living by the Raouf Pasha palace earning two percent
commission from Pierre Bardey on trade.
And when the Mahdi rose and Dervishes advanced

through Abyssinia, he mocked Kartoum's illuminated
English Gordon, rich Egyptians & the Turks,
and took a caravan of armaments on inland from Tajoura

and was ruined. He came back to Harar and tried to run
the trading station while in Paris decadents
proclaimed a system based entirely on his Sonnet of the Vowels.

Black A, white E, red I, blue O, green U.
Was he back where he belonged? This wasn't what Parnassians
had in mind. They might proclaim King Menelek

himself a symbolist if he became Negasti & Hararis were
his businessmen of Empire up and down their narrow streets.
There was no Amir left in town, no Wazir.

Sultan Ahmad bin Sultan Abibakr had asked Captain Burton
if he'd come to buy Harar. The poet advertised the sale
of priceless bodies, *hors de toute race, hors de tout monde.*

Travelers would not render their commission for a while.

She Maps Iraq

She maps Iraq. For England and for Empire
and the Man Who Would Be King.
She is Miss Gertrude Bell, a friend of T.E.L.
and Faisal. She knows much more

than all the men around her table, and she knows
they know this and despise her for her
knowledge and her fluent Arabic. They need her though,
and so she maps Iraq. They cannot find

a thing: no well or wall or wildflower blooming
where they all think nothing blooms.
What they know they only say to one another
at their club—*conceited silly flatchest windbag daughter*

of the Ironworks Bell & Bell. They'd all
sweat their smelting jealousies in Turkish baths.
She maps Iraq. They all take notes. They lean across
her table, light her endless cigarettes.

She was in love with Doughty-Wylie, Charles Doughty's
nephew who could quote in Persian poetry
that she translated back in 1893 with her lost Cadogan—
Songs of dying laughter, songs of love once warm.

Churchill sent D-Wylie to Gallipoli to die a hero and so now
she maps Iraq for Churchill, too. *And still a graver*
music runs beneath the tender love notes of
those songs she murmurs to herself, her pencil poised.

She'd loved dear old Cadogan, too, but Hugh
the foundry magnate Bell opposed a marriage with this man
of so few prospects, and she loved her brilliant father
most of all. (The gossips had her now in love with Faisal.)

At tea with Mrs. Humphrey Ward or Jenny Lind
or Henry James she used to say: *I know your work,* and
I shall go to Oxford. At Balliol, she was obliged
to sit in lectures on the history of Empire with her back

to tutor Mr. Black, and yet she got a First in spite of that,
and now she maps Iraq. There was ancient Hit
where Babylonians found oil to light their lamps. And here
was Ukhaidir, her own discovery & gift to archaeology,

or so she hoped, in photographs & sketches, measurements
of every kind. They wrote down in their notes *Petroleum at Hit*
and made no reference to the ruins at Ukhaidir.
Arabia Deserta was beside her even now, whispering

archaic Englishes that Doughty drew from Spenser,
whispering his nephew's name. She'd lead a gift-mare through
the very room and not a single hand would offer her
a sheep's eye or a carpet full of pillows on the desert sand.

She maps Iraq. She thinks their nodding heads resemble camels'
and she almost laughs remembering just yesterday
when Churchill slid from his high saddle on a camel's hump
in front of Lawrence & the Sphinx. She says that Baghdad,

Bosrah, Mosul should be *vilayets* but unified by the Sharif
the French drove out of Syria—the French, whose
archaeologists wrote up her finds at Ukhaidir before she
published *Amurath to Amurath*. The camels' heads nod on.

She says and here is Carchemish where all the Hittites
watched through their binoculars as Germans
built the Baghdad railway bridge. Had they visited
Assyrians in Kalat Shergat, all the Jewish tribes there in Haran?

She'd wager none of them had been detained by the Rashids
but she was in a harem at Hayil back when Ibn Saud marched
that way before the war. She wonders now how many of
those pills she took. Lawrence would be difficult for wives

of all these men, but she herself was thought to be impossible.
Doughty-Wiley had a wife, and so did Cox, and even
Faisal, although no one ever saw her. They said her own visits
to the sheiks were scandalous where she was treated

as an honorary man. She smoked with them and drank their
bitter coffee and could gallop their best horses
with their favorite sons. Here were twelve oases and
the routes to them and these were villages one shouldn't

for a moment underestimate. Faisal held her once so long
she felt she couldn't breathe, but then he only kissed her hand.
She still read Doughty-Wiley's letters in the night.
But where exactly draw these lines demarking Syria and

Palestine Iraq Arabia & Jordan Britain & the French had made
agreements while the Zionists had wondered was she Arab
or an English woman in her Bond Street skirts and funny hats.
It made her very tired. They said her influence had waned

but gave her titles both officially and otherwise: It was perhaps
too many of those pills she took to sleep.
She maps Iraq, but cannot now recall if in her wild travels
she had seen what she had said: *I know your work,* and

I shall go to Oxford. She was Oriental Secretary and she had
an O.B.E. She was Director of Antiquities in Baghdad
at her own museum. *And still a graver music runs beneath*
the tender love notes of those songs did not translate

Petroleum at all. She's feeling very thirsty now for water
and not oil, speaks to them of dizziness, a spell, some word
you don't pronounce as it is written or a place you've
never been that seems to be familiar as your English home.

The men stand up around her map and someone says
It isn't here and she says *but I've told you that was lost.*
Everybody leaves. They pluck their camels' heads
right off their shoulders as they go and she is back at Balliol

or in her bed and *Who said anything about Americans*
she'd give this land to Fattuh, her dear servant, or to Hugh,
her father, and you see there on her map Northumbria
is clearly inidcated as a corner of this world.

She longs for sleep in which her map would gather her
into its folds and roll her up as in a carpet taken
from the desert floor. Daughter of a foundry, she has been
a maid of Iron. For she has mapped Iraq . . .

whispers only . . . *Faisal, Fattuh, Father, take me back.*

Six Or So In Petersburg

They go out to the theatre. It's Lermontov, his Masquerade.
Shostakovich might have made an opera of it
if they hadn't executed Meyerhold. But that comes later on.
Tonight it's Meyerhold's production, it is Petersburg,
it is no ordinary evening in October. Everybody's there.

Everybody who is anyone is there. Anna Andreyevna
only managed tickets for the dress rehearsal; she isn't
anybody who is anyone just yet. The beautiful Gorenka.
When she bites her tongue she tastes her Tartar blood.
She leaves a dress shop on the afternoon it all begins.

It all begins like theatre, like Masquerade, like Lermontov.
It all begins like Meyerhold. Perhaps those mummers
mime it all, perhaps the bodies lying in the street are only
doused with buckets of red paint. The painters all come too.
The painters and the dancers and the violinists mime.

All the dead men get back up to much applause.
All the dead men lie there in the streets. Either way
the beautiful Gorenka tastes her Tartar blood & speaks.
She makes a music of this Meyerhold, this Masquerade.
The lovesick Gumilyov tells her he is dead, a suicide.

Gumilyov is not dead, he only mimes. He's shot, of course,
but that comes later on. He is in Paris, not in Petersburg.
It's Knyazev who has killed himself for love. Who will die
for Vladimir Ulyanov? Everyone who goes to Masquerade.
Gorenka has become Akhmatova. She'll write it down.

They write down everything you say. The ones who ask
you where you live, who ask your name, who ask you
why you're playing in this Masquerade. Gumilyov rides his
wayward tram back home. He cannot tell the severed heads
from cabbages with heads so cheap on sale in every shop.

They come out of the theatre and stare at all the fires.
Petersburg is burning down. It is revised, with major cuts
provided by the censors. That is, the novel by Bely.
That is, his *Petersberg*. Nikolai Apollonovich stands before
his mirror as a blood-red domino in an assassin's mask:

His hand upon a bust of Kant. The mummers in the poem
by Anna Andreyevna mime another age on the Fontanka.
She conjurs there a guest come from the future bringing doom
instead of flowers; she writes upon the writings of the dead.
There's Mandelstam; there's Meyerhold; there's Blok.

On the obverse, Pushkin's whispering *Your future is your past;
Drink the waters of Lethe.* And in her other ear the Engineer
of Souls: *Then tell us who is who and who's alive and who
is dead; we'll melt your tripple-bottomed black libretto down into
a hymn of state and gift you with a row of dots out of Onegin.*

. . .

Shostakovich plays a movement from his Seventh as the shells
explode outside his flat. He wraps himself in Gogol's overcoat
and waits for the evacuation to begin. The painters will come too.
Someone must be there to pour the blood. Beneath the window
Peter on his high bronze horse pursues the fleeing mad Evgeny.

Scherzo Trio: Three at the Villa Seurat

I HENRY

I say fuck fuck fuck fuck fuck
in all my books.
Women I call cunts and men
except for Larry all are assholes.

Eliot declares that I'm a genius
but refuses all my books at Faber.
Cancer, Capricorn, Black Spring,
you get them cheap from Obelisk.

Fuck fuck fuck fuck fuck.
You read it there in all my books:
that women all are cunts and men
except for Larry all are assholes.

II LARRY

I write heraldic prose and someone
hits upon Baroque in a review.
But I don't like Baroque; I like
bouzouki music, I like Corfu.

I'd screw Anaïs like the rest of them
if she would let me in. Why am I
the only one who doesn't get it?
I said to Henry when I met him,

You're the only one with fever'd
brain enough to see the only way
for art to go today
is straight on down the sewer!

III ANAÏS

I'm delicate, incestuous, incessant
and insane. I sleep with
all my shrinks and none of them at all
are like my famous father.

Henry's only good for once a week
but that's a great improvement on Artaud.
My diary is better than the books
by all these crooks: They will be mine forever

when all their pages have been pulped.
Fashion is as fickle as a feather.
I do say clever things. Call me from my nap
if Edmund Wilson ever rings.

Francophiles, 1958

La transhumance du Verbe, incanted René Char.
And so we would repasture
in the tower-room and try to think in French
directed by a *berger* from Morocco. Frogs were in.
Brits and Yanks were out. Hell was other people
we'd proclaim, pointing out each other's *mauvaise foi*.
What was not absurd was certainly surreal, essence rushing
headlong at existence all the way from Paris to
Vauclouse. Over hills we sent our sheep with Cathar heretics–
through unsettled valleys into settled code. (One day
predatory age would eat our lambs, but that was
too far off to see): We went to bed with both Bardot
and de Beauvoir. Fantastic volunteers of *Le Maquis*, we
knew about Algeria, about
Dien Bien Phu . . .
                    Camus was in,
Steinbeck clearly out.
Sartre had overestimated novels by Dos Pasos.
Pesos paid the wage of Sisyphus to roll
his boulder up the hill;
dollars went a good long way on continental holidays
if you could catch the Maître's mistress
mouthing his enciphered wholly unacknowledged
fully legislative & heraldic letter: *d'* . . .

But SOE and FLN were not on anybody's SATs.
No trees blossomed into Hypnos Leaves.
No one gave us arms.
No one's army occupied our town, and not
a single paratrooper dangled in his harness from our tower.
Camus declared in Stockholm: *I'm no existentialist.*
But if obliged to choose between the works
of Justice and ma mère, I will choose ma mère.

That surprised us as we greedily
claimed Justice for our own—which was easy
with our mothers safe at home & cooking us authentic dinners
that we ate like old conspirators in jails.

Still, the poet transcribed secret words
directly in his poems.
They named the roads, the villages, coordinates for
sabotage, assassination, unforeseen attacks.
We heard a beeping in the wires, the bleating
of a little flock, a change of key in those reiterations
by Ravel when music, like the Word,
tumbles starving into green transhumant fields.

Some Letters

In the end it was his daughter who would write
the book about his mother, but Wayland
fended off biographers for years after academics
on the trail of Robert Falcon Scott

trashed her on their way to the pole. It was 1980
and I lived that year at Clare Hall in Cambridge
with my wife, half-sister of Liz, wife of Wayland Young,
Lord Kennet. Wayland had been Hilton-Young at first,

like his father, Lady Scott's second husband, but he
scrapped the Hilton part when he joined the Labour Party
(at the same time, about, that Wedgwood-Benn had
smashed the Wedgwood saying, You can call me Tony).

Anyway, Wayland phoned one day and asked if I
would go identify myself at the U.L. archive and bring him
something to The Lacket, a small cottage in Wiltshire where
Lytton Strachey had written *Eminent Victorians*, I think,

sometime after Wayland's father, the first Lord Kennet,
had proposed to, and been refused by, Virginia Woolf.
He wanted the letters, deposited by him on extended loan,
that T.E. Lawrence wrote to Lady Scott after she became

a Hilton-Young and T.E.L. became a Ross, and then a Shaw.
Or was it Shaw, and afterwards Ross? I showed them my ID,
an Indiana driver's license, and they gave me a large envelope
with all the letters. I said, Can I just walk out with these?

The librarian said I could, being "Lord Kennet's representative."
So I took them to the station and caught a train for
Wiltshire, reading in astonishment Lawrence's account to
Wayland's mother, then a sculptress keen to do his bust,

about his changes in identity and habits. At one stop I got out,
Xeroxed all the letters, and caught another train.
Lawrence of Arabia! Or Shaw. Or Ross. He wrote to
Wayland's mother: "T.E. Lawrence is no more."

Wayland's mother, too, had changed from the days
when Scott would dine with her at luncheon parties that
included Barrie, Beerbohm, Isadora Duncan, Gertrude Stein.
(Peter Scott, Wayland's half-brother, had been named

for Peter Pan, a work written not in Wiltshire at the Lacket
but at Wayland's London house on Bayswater Rd.
You may have seen the blue historic plaque affixed above the door.)
When I got to the Lacket, Wayland told me that another biographer

had been in touch and that he'd grown wary, thought he'd
better see what T.E.L. had written before granting access
to the file. I gave him the originals and sat there having tea
and thinking about Lawrence, Scott, Strachey, Barrie, Beerbohm

and Virginia Woolf. After a while, Wayland leaned over
and passed me something—my driver's license, it appeared, had
been slipped by the archivist in among the letters.
Our eyes met for a moment, and I suddenly remembered all

those photocopies I had made coming down. Better burn those.
But I smiled and took the Indiana License, another cup of tea,
a scone with marmalade, and said: Lawrence of Arabia! Good Lord!
And Wayland said: Yes. A very strange little man.

From Cuttings

Goethe was impressed: he found the
plates he gazed at more exacting than
his old florilegium. These German Bauers
working off in England aimed at more
than pleasing royal patrons with the bright
and beautiful—they'd draw with great affection
even ugly weeds: also palmates & the white
clusters tinged with red and brown of an
Aesculus hippocastanum—Stubby tree he'd
drawn himself whose flower he had
pressed between the pages of a *Faust*,
whose two spiked pods he'd left in sunlight
at the corner of of his botanizing desk.
The grading of these tones. These discs & cones.
This book in which all nature was made visible
and art was all concealed . . .

His drawing, he would tell you, was today
more efficacious than his word. Still, he'd
premise his endeavors under headings
stem and *leaf* and *flower* and set you straight
about your task & his:—However short, there's
always some degree of curve in stems, and
therefore you must never use a rule; practice
at your stroke and learn to draw the parallels;
then mark off the springs of every lamina.
Blades are more or less erect and you must
draw the opposites a bit awry, and if
the stem is branched then certain leaves of course
must be foreshortened. In digitates you indicate
the petiole and midribs first to orient with

greater certainty the relative anatomies;
teeth of calyx always point between divisions
of corolla. Discriminate between a keel & wing.
And to avoid the common error perpetrated
on the flower making it put on a comic air
by twisting it upon its stalk, observe with
fierce exactitude and cultivate an equanimity.
There is no other cluster like the one you've pressed
into your book. Seed pods open.
Chestnuts. Dark eyes & a Mephistophelian look.

ENDEAVORS (2)

And Jean-Jacques Rousseau had thrown a turnip
in the face of David Hume. It made him
feel at peace, just the way that he had felt before
the Calvinists expelled him from Geneva.

Happiness had been beyond the instigators
of a lapidation that had sent him first with
gilded papers to enfold each grass and moss
and lichen on the Island of St. Peters, then
with Hume and Boswell on to Staffordshire
as refugee where there among the rocks
and sheep and rabbits he complained that he
could find no trace of scordium and had been
stoned by Hume's appalling outcry in his sleep
when they had shared a room in Roye:
Je tiens Jean-Jacques Rousseau!

Lapwings from Laputa swarmed upon him
in the Wooton fields, the meadows of Dove Dale.
The stigma was the apex of his pistil
and he'd pollinate unless he drew a breath
into his spiracle, unless he saw the eyespot there
among the algae. Insect. Eyesore. Everyone
should march along a stipule who couldn't
stipulate for any decent stipend for philosophy!
He waited for stigmata to appear. He purged
himself with tamarinds and senna, jalop
and a dash of scammony. He'd make their
lapidation lapidary, cast his own heraldic stone,
mix the henbane in the English herbal's ink.

The turnip was enough. . . . Relieved, insane,
endeavoring to float at peace upon his prose
as once he floated on his back across the waters
of St. Peter's lake, he wrote epistles to his
cousin & her daughter. *When the rays of spring*
reveal in your garden hyacinths & tulips,
jonquils & the lillies-of-the-valley, notice that the
cabbages and cole-feed, radishes and turnips
also will appear . . .

                When you find them double,
do not meddle with them for they are deformed;
nature cannot any longer live among the monsters and
the mutilated, cannot say as she was wont to say
even in the days of lapidation

Je tiens Jean-Jacques Rousseau!

Endeavors (3)

Munificence! said Dr. Robert Thornton, bowing at
the Russian's happy approbation of his work.
Alexander, Emperor and Tzar, had smiled on La Majestieuse
engraved at great expense from a painting made for
Flora's very Temple, Thornton's book, illustrated by the
author's tables and dissections, but also by the plates
that pandered to a rage for Picturesque: like Thornton's prose,
the page *majestically presented finely-polished*
bosoms to enquiring eyes.

Utile and *Dulce*, he'd insisted on them both.
Or *Dulce* first, then *Utile*. In some proportion anyway,
and no generic backgrounds for the men
to whom the likes of Mrs. Siddons sat, who was no more
than Dr. Johnson competition for a Nodding Renealmia
or Pontic Rhododendron: *no avenues of upright timber,*
gravel walks that meet by some small pond or
commonplace cascade, but scenery appropriate indeed
appropriated, brought up with the roots—

The serious roots, e.g., of Night-blowing Cereus:
Moonlight Pether's moon was told to play
on dimpled water and the Gothic turret clock to *point*
at twelve, midnight hour that finds this candle
light of orange petals at its full expanse;
Of Mimosa Grandiflora too: and Mr. Reinagle
was asked to paint *two humming birds from*
mountains in Jamaica & an aborigine who waxes all
astonished at their stationary hovering all over & about.

Dodecatheon in the Warner aquatint was blown like
Yankee Cowslip in a *gentle breeze* required also
to fill out the sails of a ship that flies the ensign
of our former colonies and waft around the specimen
indigenous and delicate bright butterflies.
Too much of something here. Or maybe not enough.
At any rate, the public did not buy. Back in Moscow
his Munificence was busy with Napoleon at the very
moment when the project needed something of a boost.

The tulips named for Earl Spencer and a duchess who
had promised patronage suddenly looked dour
and frankly parsimonious beside the open petals of
Le Roy, La Majestieuse, and La Triomphe Royale
in Earlem's greatest mezzotint. Thornton raged against
infuriate war which like devouring conflagration feasts
on commerce, agriculture and the arts, the sanguine theatre
in which the armed diffuse all rapine fire & murder and
because of which the rich are taxed beyond philanthropy.

He gazed on purple Dragon Arum and he wrote:
This foetid poisonous plant! She comes all peeping
from her purple crest with mischief fraught.
A noisome vapour issues from her nostrils and infects
the ambient air; her hundred arms are interspersed
with white as in the garments of the inquisition.
From her covert there projects a spear of darkest jet;
her sex is strangely intermingled with the opposite.
Confusion dire! Her friend is Maggot-bearing Stapelia.

I am undone by what my eyes & hands have wrought!

ENDEAVORS (4)

Although apocrypha would plant his pizzle
in the garden like a tulip bulb, the truth is that
the flower Bonaparte was known to favor
was the violet. There on Elba. Even on St. Helena.
And to the utter consternation of the English.
While the amputated bulb of his virility blossomed
in a thousand tales, the violet, much relieved,
returned to little hamlets and the village greens
in England. Sedition was no longer toasted in
the name of Corporal V or conspiracy acknowledged
Elle reparaîtra au Printemps. March violet, dog violet,
yellow violet, heart's ease: *And there is pansies,*
that's for thoughts. Who'd go a-mothering and find
the violets in the lane? Who'd strew a path to the altar,
mark a page in the book? Beyond the sickbed swelled
the purple fields. Lovers would lie down in them
and slowly braid their amulets and charms.

In 1821, the final year when Bonaparte could hope
to reappear *au Printemps,* Goethe published his objections
to the "loose concupiscence" and "constant orgies"
of the stamens & the pistils taking place among Linnaeans
who refused to propagate by morphogenesis,
and violets bloomed on every bank. Among the snow drops,
primroses, arum & anemones that marked the spring,
not a single violet grew Napoleonic;
they spread all over England as they always had.
They spread through the counties, spread through
the years, Diana raising them from Io's body
for the Father of the Gods—& also for the Slade Professor
John Ruskin who went out into his Brantwood garden

looking for a specimen in 1881.
The clump he pulled out with an angry fist
reminded him of Effie's pubic hair.

Which had annoyed him like all the prurient obscenities
that Goethe had attacked in the Linnaeans.
He wouldn't draw these flowers even for his book.
He'd rather have old Bony back.
He'd rather have his wife's pudenda smooth as petals
on a Canna Lily, hairless as a billiard ball.
He'd have her like the nine year old Miss Rose La Touche.
He wrote in *Proserpina* that *disorderly & lanky, stiff*
and springless stalks were bent in crabbed & broken
ways like spikes run up from some iron-foundry
for a vulgar railway station or like angular & dog-eared
gaspipes with their ill-hemmed leaves.
He'd have it out, he'd be entirely rid of it.
No one in the world could want to draw this clump
of flowers, *mixed together, crumpled,*
hacked about as if some cow had chewed on them
and left them tough and bitter, bad.

And she had left him years before, the marriage
quietly annulled by reason of their failure to consummate.
And Rose La Touche had died quite mad.
He was relieved, he was distraught.
He had endeavored to instruct his wife about—
it did not matter, for she would not learn.
Now he'd teach the English nation how to draw their flowers,
the English workingmen about the *Fors Clavigera*.
But there was Effie in Millais' *The Order of Release*
where every stranger in the gallery could see.
He felt imprisoned still. His stamen never

touched her pistil once. He held it in his hand
among the violets & felt like Bonaparte at Austerlitz.
Elle reparaîtra au Printemps!

ENDEAVORS (5)

To map, to classify. And that these two endeavors
are the same. Or similar. And to collect.
A kind of madness or a kindness of the sane.
And then to draw and paint what has been
mapped and classified. Why not.
And to admire that. Or not. And pay for it,
or even make it pay. Where two such endeavors are
the same, is Shelley's Lady ever present there.

In the garden there are many houses. Shall
the husbands leave them and take ship, and shall
the wives become dependent on the bees. For there
are eunuch houses where the anthers have departed
and the stamens walk a pitching deck like Captain Cook.
In what far sea. And in what key to shanty
their polygamous designs. A few hermaphrodites
were left behind when John Paxton read into the night

at Chatsworth gardens to his duke. It was a poem
in which a garden dies because some kind
of grace has been withdrawn. The Duke of Devonshire
himself was called Your Grace and thought his great
Conservatory very heaven. He'd sent his agent off
to Chirrapoonje in the Khasi hills to bring him
Amherstia nobilis for his house of glass. And he had
brought her there. He'd classified and mapped.

He'd found his way by water to Chhatak, down
the Surma River where entire trees were covered in the
epiphytes all listed in the EIC's Calcutta book, and
he had nursed, like Buddha's monks at monasteries,
tribute of a blood-red flower paid by Chirrapoonje
in the Khasi hills to Chatsworth garden and its duke
who gazed upon it while his gardener read,
sitting by his side, & while a gaudy garden died.

A Lady—the wonder of her kind, whose form was upborn
by a lovely mind, tended the garden in the poem he read.
She did not map or classify. She sprinkled water from a stream.
The duke had sent his husbands pitching on a deck.
They sang their shanties in an unknown key. The wives
became dependent on the bees while Paxton read his Shelley.
The epiphytes were listed in the book the EIC had nursed.
The duke's *Amherstia* had been acknowledged as the first

to grow in England. Never mind. Or mind. Who'd classify
and map. Who'd say that two endeavors were the same.
Who'd read aloud while Chirrapoonje drowned and grace
collected in monsoons above the Khasi hills where no one
painted and where no one drew. The duke had drawn
his household to his side to watch him sitting by his flower
while Paxton read from Shelley's poem and epiphytes grew
up Calcutta trees. The Lady sprinkled water on hermaphrodites

and spoke of no polygamous designs. The duke had asked
John Paxton for this poem. He'd sent his agent off to
Chirrapoonje in the Khasi hills; bee and mayfly kissed
the sweet lips of his flower where sanity is madness
of the kind. O Kin, the Lady was without companions
of the mortal race and yet it was as if some spirit had deserted
paradise and lingered with her there, a veil of daylight quite
concealing it from her. Or him, the duke. Who cares.

The gardener who read the poem. But no one off in
Chirrapoonje in the Khasi hills where stamens braced against
monsoons and anthers broke off in the storm. The nullas filled;
the pools flowed; the Brahmaputra delta and the Surma ran
with smallpox, ague, dysentery. Incense burned in temples
and the dung fires in wattle huts among the palms.
The crystal shattered, crystal shatters here.
The monsoon struck. Shards of glass flew everywhere

as Paxton read. Roses, figs, convolvulus had lined the banks.
The insects bred malaria. The sound of waterfalls had drowned
the cries of birds. Or not. The birdsong was so loud
it drowned the roar of waterfalls and broken glass. The Lady
listened, stopped. Rain poured through the broken roof
in torrents and the loathliest of weeds began to grow. No need
to water there where thistles, nettles, henbane, hemlock
choked the great conservatory with malignant undergrowth.

No need to map or classify or call dissimilar endeavors
much the same. No reason to collect or draw
or paint or pay for anything or try to make it pay.
A kind of madness is the kindness of the sane if only off
across the jheels you run toward Poonji like the Dawk
become a living duke. A duck perhaps. In Devonshire.
Or there in Chirrapoonje in the Khasi hills.
The Lady stared at Paxton and the poem of Shelley fills

the page with weeds. Fungi, mildew, mold began to grow
upon His Grace's cheek; a moss upon his thigh.
And hour by hour once the air was still, the vapors rose
which have the strength to kill. The baboos in Calcutta
planted seeds to cultivate the English peach and plum.
The gardener had ceased to read. The Lady now could
only plead, there in the shattered crystal house, for more.
But all was silent as it had been long before.

As Kew As You

Francis Masson in Karroo and climbing Bokkeveld
to find the *aloe dichotoma* (Dutchman's Koker Boom) of which
the Hottentots (he notes it in his diary) make quivers—
and old Mr. Frame the famous footpad still out in the sun
to take his beer at Kew whose gang might top a Florizel
outside the Drury Lane but let a thousand flowers bloom
along the green. Came Mr. David Nelson home that year
with news of Cook's dead jacknife in Hawaiian surf
came *Winter's Tale* in summer and young Perdita
the actress Mrs. Mary Robinson to fuck the Prince of Wales
for twenty thousand pounds. Lord Malden waved a handkerchief
to light the inn situated then out on the ait at Brentford.
William Aiton took the pleasure ground and measured it
for madness. Fanny Burney would attend the Queen.

Well before that measure pleasured well the footpad Frame
well both Perdita & Florizel a thousand flowers blooming there
when Cook still sailed and *aloe dichotoma* hid in Bokkeveld
the Hottentots made quivers and the consort patiently awaited
her *Strelitzia* her pretty bird of paradise and Albion especially
all the daughters fair of that same isle Professor Martyn's book:
they'd see he'd say at all times study nature & the taste of frivolous
amusements will abate it shall prevent the tumult & the passion
shall provide the mind with nourishments & all things salutary
filling it with noble objects worthy of its contemplation summer's
winter's tale will nonetheless be told dead jacknife Cook
come home a corpse the heir apparent flash a swollen stamen
from behind Lord Malden's handkerchief in androecium
and Fanny Burney to attend the scene . . . The Queen that is

no harlot nay née Charlotte Sophia of Mecklenburg-Strelitz
whose drawing-master Francis Bauer taught the ladies of
the court their parts said tip it rarely that ellipse in selfsame plane
with floret rays concavity available through all degrees
until the horizontal when your form is discoid then convex:
repeat it carpel carpellate & column innocent enough but gynoecium
with pistil pencil in and paint. Alarmed past all expression
she ran straight off with all her might but then her terror was to hear
herself pursued to hear the croaking voice of the King himself
all loud & hoarse and calling after her Miss Burney all she knew
was that the orders were to keep out of his way the garden full
of little labyrinths by which she might escape the taste of
frivolous amusements will abate it shall prevent the tumult
passion & provide for Mr. Frame the footpad in the summer sun.

No statue of Aspacia or Asoka there to hide behind she looked
askance aslant the sleeping Frame askew at such asperity
and asked him sir which herbals would be hermeneutic which ellipse
of rays medicinal although you wouldn't physically consume
an illustration of the aster for astasia. Astarte then. Austere the stare
of Reverened Mason his epistle to Sir William Chambers verses
versus Capability he'd seen untutor'd Brown destroy those wonders
from his melon ground the peasant slave had rudely rushed and
level'd Merlin's Cave knocked down the waxen wizard seized
his wand transformed to lawns what late was fairy land & marred
with impious hand each sweet design where Fanny Burney ran and
floret rays turned up at all degrees until the horizontal where the forms
became all discoid then convex the ladies sang out carpel carpellate
and column drank their gin and peered at one another's gynoecium.

West Indian planters' slaves consumed their weight in plantains why
not breadfruits from Tahiti why not send out Bligh once more
for bounty send out one more poor landlubbing botanist from Kew
to pot those plants and float a greenhouse-full some thousand miles
if convicts trod down cotyledons off in Banks' own bay conviction
had it Empire might be served by Spain's merinos bleating there by Hove
returning via Cape Town from Bombay where Francis Masson doubtless
would pass on some seed some sample of his findings old John Smeaton's
pumping engine working with an Archimedes screw some twenty-four feet
long and turned by plodding horses irrigated white house garden nicely
raising fifteen hundred hogsheads in an hour he said she said he heard
somebody say and read on in her book how there beside the Thames
sat all enthroned in vegitative pride to whom obedient sails from realms
unfurrowed brought the unnamed progeny of which she thought.

They'd name that progeny and paint it in their books who rubbed
their pates with salad oil and chased away the rooks instructing
royal nymphs fair as the Oread race who trod Europa's brink to snatch
from wreck of time each fleeting grace. Said Mr. Bauer there's not a plant
at Kew has not been drawn by you or someone of your household with
a skill reflecting on your personage but still I humbly beg you to observe
a tendency to slight the curve in stems misrepresent in leaves the midrib
where the veins must spring commit an error in perspective due to inattention
place the primrose polyanthus oxlip all of those so elementary forms right
down upon their peduncles with dislocated necks prolong a bit the stalk
or axis through the flower to the center whence the petals or divisions
may be made to radiate correctly & beyond a doubt she saw merinos that
the king had bred with convicts copulating in a bed of hyacinths
somewhere it was in lines inebriate divines had drawn or written there

or in that muck composed by Chatterton or Stephen Duck: Kew!
a happy subject for a lengthened lay though thousands write
there's something more to say thy garden's elegance thy owner's state
the highest in the present list of fate O Kew thou darling of the
tuneful nine thou eating house of verse where poets dine she drew
as best she could when Bauer asked her to respect the flower's arts
upon dissection note the size of stamens if betwixt or opposite corolla
parts and draw a line from base of filament to cleft and not regard
as trifling equanimity achieved by deftly gazing long at dried labellum
sepal stalk & style he cried for every flower blooming millions you
will understand have died a turretted and loopholed folly will be built
this very year when Captain Flinders sails out with orders straight
from Banks again to New South Wales he'll take my brother Ferdinand
along to draw those plants and animals Sir Joseph never saw.

Ah what invention graced the strain well might the laureate bard
be vain in praise of Masson in Karoo Professor Martyn's book on Kew
whose groves however misapplied to serve a prince's lust and pride
were by the Monarch's care designed a place of pleasure for the mind
they sang together every one who came to view that progeny sent back
to Kew from realms unfurrowed as the poet wrote on every sort of
frigate still afloat and Bauer took them one by one like maidens who
had been undone and spread their perianths apart to draw with all the
art he'd teach the daughters of the queen who gazed upon such colours
none of them had seen. Delineations of exotic plants and illustrations
orchidaceous taught a zygomorphic flowering flamboyant forms that
only had a precedent in certain iris norms in drawing monkey lizard bee
or spider orchid try to see the shape that looks familiar it's no jape
to say go draw a zygomorph as if it were a vegitating ape . . .

As Kew as you he heard somebody say who hid behind a bush upon
a lawn where late untutored Brown had rudely rushed and levelled
Merlin's Cave knocked down the waxen wizard seized his wand
Aspacia nor Asoka ever looked upon. As Kew as you repeated many times
the king and consort poets and divines a drawing master Perdita
the Prince of Wales those friends of Mr. Frame still languishing in jails
and those just back from Cape Town or Bombay as Kew as you
the hours that every day the sundials clocked along the garden walk
where Fanny Burney liked to sit and talk or write down in her book
as Kew as you would caw the captain's rook advancing on a bishop
over board at sea en route to bring back yet more loot and plants named
for the Englishmen who sought them out as Kew as you for botanists
to tout & draw transplant dissect in all the ways Sir Joseph would direct
as Kew as you ... he'd tell them every one exactly what to do.

Part VI

From A Compostela Diptych

For John Peck and Guy Davenport

I

Via Tolosona, Via Podiensis.
There among the tall and narrow cypresses,
the white sarcophagi of Arles

worn by centuries of wind & sun,
where Charlemagne's lieutenants it was said
lay beside Servilius & Flavius

and coffins drifted down the Rhone
on narrow rafts to be unloaded by St. Victor's monks,
they walked: Via Tolosona.

Via Podiensis: They walked as well from
Burgundy through the Auvergne,
slogged along volcanic downland up into Aubrac

and on through Languedoc to Conques
and gazed into the yellow morning light falling
from above the central axis through

the abbey's lantern tower
and praised St. Foy, and praised as well
with Aimery Picaud their guide

the names of certain travelers
who had long before secured the safety of their way
and also other ways: Via Podiensis,

Via Lemosina, Via Turonensis.
They crossed the Loire at Tours and at Nevers,
walking toward Bordeaux or

from St. Leonard and St. Martial of Limoges
to Périgord and to Chalosse.
At Tours beside the sandy, wide & braided river

they would rest a while and bathe
or seek the narrow shoals nearby & shallow streams
that ran between. Here St. Martin's

shrine had outfaced Abd-al-Rahman
and they prayed at his basilica remembering
the ninety thousand Moors

beaten back to Córdoba before Almansor
took the bells of Santiago
for his candle-sticks, hung them highly

in his elegant great mosque & upside down.
His singers sang of it.
These walking also sang: Via Lemosina,

Via Turonensis: they sang the way along the ways.
They sang the king: *Charles li reis,*
ad estet en Espaigne ... Tresqu'en la mer

conquiste la terre altaigne. Trouvères, jongleurs,
langue d'oïl, lanque d'oc: of love
& war, the Matamoros & the concubine at Maubergeon.

And there was other song—song sung inwardly
to a percussion of the jangling
manacles and fetters hanging on the branded

heretics who crawled the roads
on hands and knees and slept with lepers under
dark facades of abbeys

& the west portals of cathedrals with their zodiacs.
These also sang: as had
the stern young men, their sheep or cattle

following behind, when up
to high summer pasture they would carry
from the scoria-red waste

a wooden image of their black and chthonic mother
burned in her ascent up out of
smoking Puy-de-Dome (or her descent

from very heaven: Polestar's daughter urging
them to Finisterre. . . .
                              Whichever way

they came they sang.
Whatever song they sang they came.
Whichever way they came, whatever song they sang,

they sang and walked together on the
common roads: Via Lemosina,
Via Turonensis; Via Tolosona, Via Podiensis.

II

Dorian, Phrygian, Lydian—
modes in diatonic sequence which would order
the response & antiphon at Cluny:

authentic, plagal; plagal and authentic—
hypodorian, hypomixolydian—
Magnificat! Magnificat anima mea Dominum.

And canticles in stone carved in capitals
to honor every mode
in which the honor of this Lady might

be chanted, melismatic even,
graced the choir itself in St. Hugh's hall
where someone wrote the book

sending walkers down the roads to Santiago.
Whose creation Aimery Picaud?
Whose persona Turpin? *The Codex Calixtinus!*

Book that wrought a miracle of power?
or book that answered it and echoed it, reflected
power trans-Pyrenean and uncanny,

causality determined by no human hand?
Did Santiago draw his pilgrims to his shrine,
or did the Monks of Cluny push?

Far from the basilica, far from
the *corona* with its hundred lamps & more lighted
there to brighten Pentecost or Easter, far

from the twelve arcades of double pillars,
the goldsmith's workshop & the bearded lutenist beside
the dancing girl celebrating in their frozen

artistry the artistry of monophonic provenance
which answered every gesture
of the vestured celebrant—and far, far before

the carving of a single capital,
the scribbling of a single line of Latin in a single book,
the hammering of gold, the glazing

of an ornament, the singing of the kyrie or gloria,
the censing of the host,
a strange boat arrived off Finisterre. . . .

(Or so they say. Or so they said
who made the book.) The boat came from Jerusalem
without a sail, without a rudder,

without oars. It bore his head beside his body
who had caught it when the sword
of Herod dropped it in his open hands.

It bore his two disciples. As they neared
the land beneath the *campus stellae*
where the lord of every geste would heave his

spear into the surf, drawn across the Pyrenees
by virtue of this other who would lie down now
for some eight hundred years—son of Zebedee

and Salomé, brother of St. John, son of Thunder
born into Galicia—
a bridegroom riding to his wedding reined

his horse in, stared a moment at the little boat,
galloped straight into the tranquil sea.
When horse and rider rose, both were covered with

the scallop shells that were his sign, his
awaiting Cluny and his cult
(the carving of the capitals, the canticles in stone,

the singing of the antiphons,
the scribbling of the Latin in his lenten book)
but also *hers*—

Magnificat! Magnificat anima mea Dominam—
who rose up on a scallop shell
to dazzle any bridegroom staring at whatever sea.

So it began. So they said it had begun.
A phase (a phrase (a moment in
the spin of some ephemeride (a change

not even in the modes of music
from the Greek
to the Gregorian. . . .

   (And chiefly with an aim to rid the south of Moors, to rid it of
the Mozarabic taint in liturgies and chants, to blast the peasant
heretics following the Gnostic light of Avila's Priscillian. And
then? Then the castigations of Bernard, the smashings of the
Huguenots, the marshals of Napoleon on the mountain trails, the

slow dismantling of the abbey for its stone, the twists of floral
patterns on the the broken columns standing in the ruined gran-
ary, the Shell Oil station on the highway through the pass. And at
the restaurant by the river in St-Jean-Pied-de-Port (Michelin: 2
stars), good coquilles St. Jacques . . .

V

Aoi.
Pax vobiscum, pax domini,
Aoi.
     Ainsi soit il.

And Charles murdered fourteen hundred Saxons
after Roncevaux, cutting off their heads,
when no one would reveal the hiding place of

Widukind, when no one would convert. A northern
paradigm for slaughters in the south?
At the far end of the trail, before there was a trail,

there were tales told: narratives of gnosis
whispered themselves north
to bleed in Roussillon when shepherds saw the

flocks of transmigrating souls walk among their
sheep looking for good company
and habitation. . . .
           Even thus Galicia's Priscillian:

Executed 385 by Evodius, Prefect appointed
by the tyrant Maximus,
at the urging of Ithacius, his fellow Bishop....

The soul, then, of its own will doth come to earth,
passing through the seven heavens, and
is sown in the body of this flesh. Or would one rather

say, as did Orosius to St. Augustine: "Worse than
the Manichees!" And the Saint: "Light!
which lies before the gaze of mortal eyes, not only

in those vessels where it shines in its purest state,
but also in admixture to be purified:
smoke & darkness, fire & water & wind . . . its own abode."

Along the Via Tolosona to Toulouse and then beyond
they told the tales: tunics of human flesh,
penitential wandering, sparks hereticated, vestures of decay.

They praised the seal of the mouth,
the seal of the belly and the hand; the demiurge
was author of this world;

among the rocks and trees, among the sheep
& cattle, they acknowledged each
the aeon that was only an apparent body, only born

apparently into the pitch and sulphur of a human shape
to utter human words. The words
they uttered and the tales they told were strange:

. . . when I was once
a horse, I lost my shoe between
the stones & carried on unshod the whole night long.

Cloven to the navel by this wound got of a Moor,
I speak to him alone who goes out
with the dead, the messenger of souls

who saw the lizard run into the ass's skull. . . .
the Ram presides above the head,
The Twins behind the loins. . . .
                          Were these voices then

an echo of a field of force counter to
the leys on which the houses of St. James aligned
themselves from north of Arles into Spain?

No Cluniac reform or Romanesque adornment to
the dogma from the rustic prentices of old Priscillian
dead eight hundred years before their time;

no chant in diatonic mode, in good Gregorian, but
diabolic danger here. This
called out for Inquisition and for blood.

Across all Occitania, across the Languedoc
and down the Via Tolosona spread
the news: Béziers was ruined and destroyed,

fifteen thousand fell before the walls & in the town
where mercenaries heard the knights cry out
to conjure holocaust: *kill them all; God will know his own.*

At Bram, Monfort gouged the eyes out, cut
the nose and upper lip off all survivors of his siege,
leaving just one man with just one eye

to lead his friends to Cabaret.
This was orthodox revenge. This was on the orders
of a man called Innocent.

Raymond of Toulouse, driven from his city,
fled to England, then returned
through Spain where troops passed down the Somport Pass

along the Tolosona to link up with his confederates,
the counts of Foix and of Comminges.
The chronicles explain that *everyone began*

to weep and rushed toward Raymond as he entered
through the vaulted gates to kiss
his clothes, his feet, his legs, his hands.

He appeared to them like one arisen from the dead.
At once the population of the town
began to mend the walls that Monfort had torn down.

Knights and burgers, boys and girls, great and small,
hewed and carried stones while troubadours
sang out their mockery of France, of Simon, of his son.

It was not enough. Though Simon died
outside the walls, the French king and Pope Honorious
concluded what the Monforts

and Pope Innocent began. Behind the conquerors
there came Inquisitors, with
the Inquisitors, denunciations, torture and betrayal.

But in the mountains and along the shepherd's paths
leading to and from the Tolosona trail,
the old tales nonetheless were whispered still

far from cities and the seneschals, far from
Bernard Gui, his book & his Dominicans.
The cycle of transhumance led itinerant *perfecti*

there among gavaches as far from their own ostals
as the Ariège is from Morella,
the wide Garonne from Ebro's northern bank & winter camp.

. . . tunics of human flesh,
penitential wandering, sparks hereticated, vestures
of decay. . . .

Among the rocks and trees, among the sheep
and cattle, they acknowledged each
the aeon that was only an apparent body, only born

apparently into the pitch & sulphur of a human shape
to utter human words.
And in Galicia, beneath the nave, restless with the centuries,

the east-facing tombs out of all alignment with
the Roman mausoleum & supporting walls
take up proximity below the bones in Santiago's vault

to something holy. The martyred heretic of Trier?
Aoi.
Pax vobiscum, pax domini.

    Aoi. Ainsi soit il.

    VI

But was it this that found the floriations
in the columns, found in capitals
the dance that found the music of the cloister & the choir,

the song that found the south for Eleanor of Aquitaine?
Trobar, they said: to find.
To find one's way, one's path, to find the song,

to find the music for the song,
to find through stands of walnut, poplar, chestnut,
through meadows full of buttercups

and orchids, over or beside the banks of many rivers
from above Uzerche to well below
the Lot—Vézère, Corrèze, Couze, Dordogne, Vers—

along the paths of sandstone, rust red & pink,
the way through Limousin, through Perigord, all along
the Via Lemosina to a small road leading to

a castle gate, to find a woman in that place
who finds herself in song,
to find a friend, a fellow singer there or on the road.

Or to the north and west, at Poitiers,
along the Touronensis after
Orléans and Tours, to find before the heaths

of Gascony the pine forests and the *plat pays*
of Poitevins who speak the language
sung by William, Lord of Aquitaine, or the Lemosin

of singers who found comfort who found welcome
at his son's court, his who died
at Santiago, and the court of Eleanor his heir

whose lineage from Charlemagne found Angevin Bordeaux.
They came from Albi and Toulouse,
the town of Cahors and the county of Quercy,

but did they find for her and sing
the *Deus non fecit* of the heretic *perfecti* of Provence
or the Light from Eleusis

bathing trail and keep and column in its warmth?
Beneath the limestone cliffs of the Dordogne,
past the verges bright with honeysuckle, thyme and juniper,

quarried stone and timber floated toward the sea
on barges by the dark ores of the *causse,*
while salt, fish, and news of Angevin ambition & desire

came on inland from Bordeaux and from Libourne.
From Hautefort, Ribérek; from
nearby Ventadorn, singers found their way to Poitiers.

The sun rains, they sang: *lo soleils plovil,*
while pilgrims in Rocamadour
climbed toward what they sought, singing without benefit

of trobar ric or trobar clus: *midonz, midonz*
in a dazed vision of the lady there,
hunched & black upon a stick fallen from the sky.

To sing, to pray: to find behind them
south of Ventedorn, of Hautefort, of Cahors & Toulouse,
alignments in the temple of the sun

at Montségur measuring the solstice, measuring
the equinox, dawn light raining
through the eastern portholes of a ship

riding its great wave, counting down the year,
counting down the years, sign by sign
from Aries to The Fish, not to brighten only that

new morning in Provence but latterly to bend
also onto any path
of any who would follow, singing

at the gates of abbeys or below the castle walls
in any language found
where every song was fond

and yet forbidding, forensic as the night.
Did those who sang, do those who sing,
care at all that at the ending of their song,

as at the start, William of Aquitaine,
son of the troubadour, father of the child
they would hail in Poitiers

kneels crying *midonz* to the stars
but finds in Santiago's tomb not the bones of James
but those of the heretic Priscillian?

I am Arnaut who gathers the wind.
I am Arnaut who hunts the hare with the ox.
I am Arnaut who swims against the tide.

    ∼

Near Excidieul, long after Aquitaine
was France, after the end
of what was Angevin, and after the end of the end,

two lone walkers slogged along the road
and spoke of vortices
and things to be reborn

   after Europe's latest conflagration. Was it spring? Was it 1920?
The older of the two, trying to remember after fifty years, could not
be sure. It was he who had crept over rafters, peering down at the
Dronne, once before. He knew that Aubeterre was to the east, that
one could find three keeps outside Mareuil, a pleached arbour at
Chalais. He knew the roads in this place. He had walked into
Perigord, had seen Narbonne, Cahors, Chalus, and now was once
again walking with his friend near Excidieul. In certain ways he
much resembled the old finders of song, and sang their songs in
his own way and tried to make them new. He called the other one,
his friend, Arnaut, though that was not his name, and stopped

with him beside a castle wall. He saw above them both, and wrote down in his book, *the wave pattern cut in the stone, spire-top alevel the well curb,* and then heard this other say, the sun shining, the birds singing, *I am afraid of the life after death.* Of a sudden. Out of the calm and clarity of morning.

He stored the loved places in his memory—the roads, the keeps beside the rivers, the arbour at Chalais—and walked in Eleusinian light and through the years to Rimini and Rome, in darkness on to Pisa in another war. And after fifty years, and from the silence of his great old age, he said: *Rucksacked, we walked from Excidieul. When he told me what he feared, he paused and then he added:* "Now, at last, I have shocked him. . . . "

Who was Arnaut to gather the wind?

INTERCALATION

And who, asked the Doctor Mellifluus, were the Cluniacs to gather all *these* things: *deformis formositas ac formosa deformitas.* A wave pattern cut in the stone would have been enough—would have been, perhaps, too much. But apes and monstrous centaurs? half-men and fighting knights? hunters blowing horns? many bodies under just one head or many heads sprouting from a single body? Who were the Cluniacs to gather round them windy artisans to carve their curiosities, to carve chimeras, onto cloister capitals from St. Hugh's Hall to Santiago so that it became a joy to read the marbles and a plague to read the books. The concupiscence of eyes! For he had deemed as dung whatever shone with beauty. (Dung, too, was music and the talk, *humanus et jocundus,* of the monks, or the song of deeds in poetry. The concupiscence of ears! For he'd have silence, silence, save when he would speak, the great voice shaking his emaciated frame near to dissolution and yet echoing through all of Christendom: *Jihad! Jihad!* He looked upon the mind of Abelard, the body of Queen Eleanor, and did not like them. Man of the north, he gazed upon the south and built the rack on which they'd stretch the men of Languedoc after he'd made widows of the women standing horror-stricken outside Vézelay the day a thousand knights called out for crosses.) Contra Dionysius, the pseudo-Areopagite. Contra Saint-Denis. Contra Grosseteste, contra Bonaventure, and before their time. There was, he thundered, darkness in the light. And light in darkness of the fastness, of the desert, of the cave.

And yet, Abbot Suger sighed, thinking of his Solomon and walk-ing in the hall the saint had called the Workshop of Vulcan, the Synagogue of Satan: *dilectio decoris domus Dei. . . . Cross of St. Eloy! Thy chrysolite, thy onyx and thy beryl.* It seemed to him he dwelt in some far region of the mind not entirely on this earth nor yet

[285]

entirely in the purity of Heaven. . . . When he looked upon such stones. . . . When the sun's rays came flooding through the windows of the choir. For he was servant to the Pater Luminum and to the First Radiance, his son. Their emanations drenched so utterly this mortal world that, beholding them polluted even in the vestures of decay, we should rise—*animae*—by the manual guidance of material lights. The onyx that he contemplated was a light, the chrysolite a light, lights the screen of Charlemagne, the Coupe de Ptolemées, the crystal vase, the chalice of sardonyx, and the burnished ewer. Also every carving in the stones—the capitals, the portal of the west facade—and every stone itself, placed with cunning and with reverence according to the rules of proportion on the other stones, and then proportion too, laws invisible made visible by building—place and order, number, species, kind—these were lanterns shining round him which, he said, *me illuminant.*

But to Citeaux, but to Clairvaux: letters which began *Vestra Sublimitas* (and without irony). Acknowledging intemperance in dress, intemperance in food and drink; acknowledging the horses fit for kings and their expensive, sumptuous liveries; superfluities of every kind, excesses which endangered everything, opening the Royal Abbey to the winds of calumny. . . . He'd move into the smallest cell. He'd walk while others rode. He'd fast. . . . And yet expand the narthex and reconstruct the choir. Enlarge and amplify the nave. Find a quarry near Pontoise in which they'd cut no longer millstones for their livelihood but graceful columns by the grace of God. He'd execute mosaics on the tympanum, elaborate the crenellations. Hire castors for the objects to be bronzed, sculptors from the Cluniacs to carve in columns tall figures on the splayed jambs. Abolish compound piers and redesign triforia. Raise the towers up above the rose making of the rose itself a fulcrum. Repair the lion's tail that supported until recently the collonette. Repair zodiacal reliefs and, in the crypt, the capitals' eight abacus athemia. In the

Valley of Chevreuse, he'd hunt himself for twelve tall trees, trunks sufficient in their height for roof-beams of his new west roof and fell them in the woods with his own axe, and offer thanks. Nor would he renounce the light—whatever letters went off to Bernard of Clairvaux—the light proportionate unto itself, order mathematical of all diffusion, infinite in volume and activity, lux and lumen both.

And then at Vézelay, Bernard. Sunny Burgundy. The Via Podiensis and the city on the hill. Bishops, statesmen, peasants hungry for some kind of fair, thugs and mercenaries, Louis King of France who ached for glory and beside him Eleanor. Multitudes so many that they flooded all the fields waiting for the prophet from Clairvaux who would command them (Suger quiet under some far tree; Suger strong for peace). At Sens, he had destroyed Abélard. Now he'd widow all the women of the north. Rhetorician of the Holy War, demagogue of the crusade, he stood outside the abbey where the Pentecostal Christ of Gislebertus, *sol invictus* of the entry to the choir, measures time. But then what time was *this*, what year? Sea-green incorruptible beneath his Abbot's shroud, he numbered hours and souls in strict and occult symmetry. Were days measured once again by Kalends, Nones and Ides? Was solstice equinox and equinox the solstice? Did lunar phases intersect the solar year? Who had carved a column with the *lam* and *alif* of the Holy Name and was it *zenith* now or *nadir* in the Latin's Arabic? Many bodies sprouted from his head and many heads from every weaving body. Hautbois and bass bombarde began to play, shawm and chime and rebec as the voices sang *Fauvel* and *Reis Glorios*. From Mont Saint-Michel to Sens, from Besançon to Finisterre, a darkness fell at noon, the walls of houses cracked, down from all the bell towers tumbled bells. In a far encampment, flames leapt from spears of ash and apple, hauberks buckled, steel casques burst, bears and leopards walked among the men in Bernard's dream. For so he dreamed, even as he spoke. Dreamed within a dream Jerusalem's high requiem before the ships of Saladin sailed south from Tyre, their mastheads and their prows decked and lighted through the night with lamps and rubies in the story that the emirs tell. But everything would not be done at once. He saw emblazoned on a calendar suspended in the sky that it would be the year of Grace—but it would be no year of Grace when he awakened from his grave and found the month Brumaire: Those before him in the field walked straight over his indignant ghost and, shouting out obscenities, burned and looted in the abbey, then marched back down Via Podiensis and the Rue St. Jacques into the capital. All of Paris quaked beneath the church of St. Denis and night revealed itself in which the very stars went out as mobs broke in to take the challices, the vials, the little golden vessels used to serve the wine of the ineffable First Light, and swilled their brandy from those cups, then with clubs and hammer beat them flat. Long lines of priests in vestments led through burning streets a train of mules and of horses laden with patinas, chandeliers and censers from a dozen churches on the Santiago trail, pushed before them carts and wheel-barrows loaded with ciboriums and candle-sticks and silver suns. *Merde!* they shouted. *Vanities!* And tore from roofs and crannies sculpted figures wearing crowns to smash their eyes out and their jaws into a stony chorus of eternal silent screams. Relics torn from reliquaries fed the bonfires and the holy dead themselves were disinterred. Bells from Languedoc, from Conques, bells that rang above him there at Vézelay, were melted down for cannon and the cannon dragged along the trails into Spain to blast the columns and the capitals, the arms and legs and heads of kingdom come, into the brain of Goya—Vézelay's splayed Christ upon the door become the victims of the Tres de Mayo, the *deformis formositas ac formosa deformitas* of the twisted and uncanny *Disparates,* the black figures on El Sordo's Quinta walls.

... how many years?
The Abbot Suger did not know, but he was Regent.
He set about his work.

Pilgrims set off walking down the Via Podiensis from the church
    of Julien le Pauvre.

Part II: Spain

   I

And from the ninety-second year of the Hegira
and from Damascus
and from the lips of Caliph Walid Abulabas:

permission for Tariq ibn-Ziyad to set forth
from Ceuta in his borrowed ships
to see if what was spoken by Tarif ibn Malik

and his captives of al-Andalus
was true: serene skies, an excellence of weather,
abundant springs and many rivers,

fruit & flowers & perfume as fine as in Cathay,
mines full of precious metals, tall
standing idols of Ionians amidst extraordinary ruins,

and an infidel weak king despised by tribes & peoples
who but waited to be rendered tributary
to the Caliphate and subject to Koranic law.

And then: collapse of Visigothic armies

at the battle near Sierra de Retín,
knights' bodies tossed into the rising Barbate

and the footmen with their slings & clubs & scythes
falling before Berber scimitars
days before the Qaysite and Yemeni horsemen

under Musa ibn-Nusayr could even cross
from Jabal Musa. Then the hurried crossing of the straight,
the meeting between Musa and Tariq at Talavera,

the occupation of León, Astorga, Saragossa,
and the messenger prostrate before the Caliph in Damascus
saying *Yes! Serene skies, an excellence of weather,*

abundant springs and many rivers, fruit and flowers
and perfume as fine as in Cathay,
mines full of precious metals and, inside this bag

I open for you now, O Caliph,
the severed head of Roderick, king of the Visigoths.
Behold the token of our victory!

Died al-Walid Abulabas in the ninety-sixth year
of the Hegira when, for his troubles,
Musa was condemned by Sulayman to prison & the bastinado

and Tariq ibn-Ziyad disappeared from every chronicle.
But the chronicles themselves go on:
A bad time for Umayyads at home, but every

kind of glory for the jihad in al-Andalus.
Which is why the hungry Umayyad, hunted in the the streets
and alleys by the Abbasids, was going there:

the young man hiding in the rushes of Euphrates,
then a silhouetted horseman riding through the desert in the
        night,
the moon on his shoulder, the pole star in his eye.

Landing north of Málaga, he wrote his laws.
Having *crossed the desert*
& the seas & mastered both the wasteland & the waves,

he came into his kingdom, for he was Abd-al-Rahman
and would rule: *no one*
to be tortured, no one to be crucified or burned,

separated from his children or his wife, or anyone
to be despoiled of his holy objects
if in tribute come the golden dinars & the golden wheat

the flour & the barley heaped in bushels on the wagons
to be weighed, the measures
requisite of vinegar and honey, common musk & oil.

And Abd-al-Rahman rebuilt the mosque in Córdoba.
And the second Abd-al-Rahman
Gathered the philosophers and poets, gathered the musicians

and the concubines and wives. And the Sufi at the gates
called his heart a pasture for gazelles, said
he'd come to Córdoba following the camels of his love.

From the columns left by Rome there sprouted upwards
palm-like in oasis the supports
for Allah's double tier of arches, hemisphere

upon the square, fluted dome upon the vault. . . .
When they built the Alcázar &
Madinat al-Zahra, six thousand dressed stones

were called for every day, 11,000 loads of lime & sand.
There were 10,000 workmen, 12,000 mules.
By their kilns and pits, the potters & the tanners,

the armorers and smiths. . . . Plane, then, on plane . . .
the surface of each building there
a depth of arabesque, brick and faience overlaid

with geometric pattern & the forms of Kufic & Basmala
lettering interlaced with flowers,
framed by grape vine and acanthus all dissolving

strength & weight & structure in a dazzle of idea:
horror vacui: shifting ordering of order
all unseen, water of icosahedron, air of octahedron

fire of tetrahedron on the simple cube of earth,
living carpet in the grid of pathways behind walls,
sunken flower-beds, myrtle bushes

shading tributaries of the central pool and reflection
of the zones and axes of this world
crossing at the intersection where a Ziryab might play

his lute or al-Ghazal recite. . . . And Abd-al-Rahman
built on Abd-al-Rahman's work, &
Abd-al-Rahman brought it to completion. . . .

Who could have forseen in these expansive years
the squabbling of *taifas*
and Moorish rulers paying tribute to

Alfonso, Sancho, & Rodrigo Díaz El Campeador?
No one walked along the roads
to cross the Aragón where every route converged upon

a single bridge or sang the tales of El Cid & Charlemagne
slogging through Navarre into Castile.
But it was spring. Spring in Burgundy and spring

in all al-Andalus. In Cluny & in Córdoba they carved
stones and sewed the mint & the marjoram;
silkworms hatched & beans began to shoot and all

the apple & the cherry trees flowered white at once.
Water in the aqueducts was fresh as snow
in mountain streams, & everything it irrigated green.

But when the Sufi heard the flute notes in the air
and his disciples asked him
Master, what is that we hear outside the wall?

he looked up from the pile of sand on which he sat
reading the Koran and said:
It is the voice of someone crying for this world

because he wishes it to live beyond its end.
He cries for things that pass.
Only God remains. The music of the flute

Is the song of Satan crying in the desert
for the wells that all run dry,
for the temples & the castles & the caliphates that fall.

IV

Oit varones una razón! he shouted
in the dusty square,
echoing the *Hoc Carmen Audite* of certain Joculatores,

Joculatores Domini, who stepped around him
and his eager rabble of an audience
to walk beneath the scaffold of the master of Sangüesa

who would freeze him there forever in the stone
even as he left the town
to sing the wayfarers upon their way

from Yesa on through Burgos to León.
On the portal he disports himself with viol & bow,
and also with the lady in a sexy gown

whose other friend is farting in a well beside a cooper
struggling with his heavy barrel.
But on the trail he was quintessential news, was history itself,

and sang the life of Don Rodrigo while El Cid
yet earned the fame to warrant song.
And aged within his story. And grew so very old

his song became a banner among banners
of reconquest: *Oit varones*
una razón—of reconciliation on the Tagus, it might be,

once the hero halted at El Poyo,
once the heralds brought him followers from Aragón & Monreal,
once Minaya sought Alfonso for him

west in Sahagún, west in Carrión,
toward which they walked who'd gathered in the square
beneath the portal of María la Real.

And when Rodrigo rode to meet his king the villagers
& peasants saw, the singer sang
tanta buena arma, tanto buen cavallo corredor—

splendid weapons, swift horses, capes and cloaks
and furs and everyone
vestidos son de colores, all dressed in colors,

underneath the banners
when he stopped on the Tagus, when he fell upon
his face before Alfonso, when he

took between his teeth the grasses of the field—
las yerbas del campo—and wept
great tears as if he had received a mortal wound

and would be reconciled with the earth itself. . . .
as act of faith? Auto de fé?
& near the Tagus once again, Toledo's banners flying

long long beyond him who had come to meet Alfonso
from Valencia & him whose song
became a banner among banners of reconquest?

This *razón* was also sung along the trails, for it was news,
and it was news of conflagration
great as that which burned the northern cities

in the Caliphate: this *razón* was Torquemada's song.
Hoc Carmen Audite.
In conspecto tormentorum . . . (as when Don Rodrigo's daughters

lash and spurs were shown by their own bridegrooms.
When they entered the grove of Corpes
following the two Infantes back to Carrión near Sahagún.

. . . *bien lo creades*
aquí seredes escarnidas en estos fieros montes.
Oy nos partiremos . . .

And they knew it for a certainty that they
would be tormented
scourged and shamed and left in that dark place.)

Those abjuring marched with tapers through each town
& wore the sambenito & the yellow robe
embroidered with a black Saint Andrew's cross.

The crier walked before them, crying out
to those who came to watch
the nature of offenses to be punished while

behind them came the paste-board effigies
of those Marranos and Moriscos
who had died of torture, and exhumed bodies

of the heretics dead & buried before Torquemada
reigned at every quemadero:
Hoc Carmen Audite. In conspecto tormentorum. . . .

These we order vicars, rectors, chaplains, sacristans
to treat as excommunicated & accursed for
having now incurred the wrath & indignation of Almighty God

& on these rebels & these disobedient
be all the plagues and maledictions which befell upon
king Pharaoh and his host & may

the excommunication pass to all their progeny.
May they be accursed in eating
& in drinking, in waking and in sleeping,

in coming and in going. Accursed be they
in living & in dying & the devil
be at their right hand; may their days be few

and evil, may their substance pass to others,
may their children all be orphans & widows all their wives.
May usurers take all their goods;

May all their prayers be turned to maledictions;
accursed be their bread and wine,
their meat and fish, their fruit & any food they eat;

the houses they inhabit & the raiment that they wear.
Accursed be they unto Satan
and his lords, & these accompany them both night & day. . . .

But far from Toledo, on the road to Sahagún & Carrión,
they told the tales: tunics of human flesh,
penitential wandering, sparks hereticated, vestures of decay.

They praised the seal of the mouth,
the seal of the belly and the hand; the demiurge
was author of this world;

among the rocks and trees, among the sheep
& cattle, they acknowledged each
the aeon that was only an apparent body, only born

apparently into the pitch and sulphur of a human shape
to utter human words. And the Jews
hid their secret practices, and the Arabs likewise theirs,

and at the ending of the song, as at the very start,
Don Rodrigo asked his king,
earning thus his exile: *Did you kill your brother?*

Did you collude & commit incest with your sister?
For if you did, all your schemes will fail,
even though I lie prostrate before you eating grass. . . .

Take this oath upon the iron bolt, upon the crossbow.
Otherwise, may peasants murder you—
Villanos te maten, rey; villanos, que no hidalgos;

even though I lie prostrate before you eating grass. . . .

~

When the singer reached the bridge at Puente la Reina
with the pilgrims who had followed him
for some six hundred years, they met an army:

Soult and Ney & other marshals of Napoleon crossing
into Spain through Roncevaux
and trailing all the engines of their empire. . . .

. . . bien lo creades
aquí seredes escarnidas en estos fieros montes.
Oy nos partiremos. . . .

Aoi.
Oit varones una razón.
Aoi.

Hoc Carmen Audite.

V

Soult was at Saldaña on the Carrión
when General Stewart's aide-de-camp walked into Rueda
past the cow-dung fires of peasants

to discover there some eighty horsemen who belonged,
he ascertained, to a division of
Franceski's cavalry. These the light dragoons surrounded

after midnight. General Moore advanced from Salamanca
through Alaejos to Valladolid, & a stolen
sabretache with full intelligence in Marshal Berthier's dispatch

revealed that Junot's infantry had yet to cross the Ebro
and that Ney was still engaged at Saragossa.
On forced march, the British trod December's icy roads

from Toro to Mayorga south of Sahagún.
What pilgrims they became!
Everyone a step-child to some devotee of Sol Invictus,

god of legionaries in whatever expeditionary war,
they billeted beneath the frieze
of Saint María del Camino with its bulls' heads

on abutments of the inner arch, racing horsemen,
and a naked rider on a lion.
They'd drag like Mithra in a week their burdens

down unholy trails and over mountains to the cave
that was Coruña. Exactly where the spears
of Charlegmagne's unburied dead had sprouted leaves

along the Cea at the edge of Sahagún, they halted
their advance. By Alfonso's grave,
by the graves of Doña Berta & Constanza, his French queens,

by the ruins of the abbey that had rivaled Cluny
built by Jaca's Englishman
where Aimery Picaud had found unrivalled natural beauty

and a city radiant with grace,
these Englishmen of Sir John Moore's found news:
that Bonaparte himself had crossed the Duoro

and would crush them where they were or drive them
to the sea. They turned and fled;
joined a procession of the living and the dead.

Before them, taurophorus, Mithra dragged the bull,
took its hooves upon his shoulders,
pulling it up mountain trails after Villafranca

in the sleet and snow. Behind them, in his death,
embalmed Rodrigo—tied to beams
that braced him in his saddle, dressed for combat,

sword in hand, looking like some exhumed agent
of the Holy Office driving
heretics to the new trans-Cantabrian quemaderos. . . .

. . . *tantas lanças premer e alçar,*
tanta adágara foradar e passar. . . . *tanta loriga*
falssar e desmanchar, tantos pendones

salir vermejos en sangre. . . . lances, bucklers,
coats of mail broken there,
pennons of the foreign legions soaked in blood . . .

If Suero de Quiñones read aloud the twenty-two
conditions of the tournament
in which he'd win his ransom at the Orbiego bridge

and then proclaim the Paso Honroso,
who would answer for these blood-shod infantry between
Bembibre and the Cua not *Oit Varones* . . .

but *Ahora sueña la razón?*
If reason dreamt on this retreat, then so did song.
It slept and dreamed its monsters

in the language of a soldiery that spat and swore
cursing all the bridges
that would measure honor & had measured piety before.

No one shouted *Vivan los Ingleses* as they passed
through villages to loot & rape
where church bells rang when they had gone to summon Soult.

Stragglers broke into bodegas, smashed the wine casks,
then cut up the dying mules & bullocks
by the roadside that had pulled artillery & ammunition vans

to boil them in kettles on great fires they built with gun butts
and mix with what remained of issue brandy,
salted meats and biscuits and the buckets full of melted snow.

Those who dared to sleep were frozen dead by morning,
and when chasseurs came in twos & threes
to scout the strength of Moore's rear guard, they hacked

the arms off those who staggered in the wind
or split their heads down to their chins with sabers flashing
in the sun. All the rest was in the hills.

From Villafranca to Nogales, from
Nogales on through Lugo to Betanzos, darkness fell at noon,
the walls of houses cracked, down

from all the bell towers tumbled bells.
On the march, flames leapt from spears of ash & apple,
hauberks buckled, steel casques burst,

bears and leopards walked among the men
in John Moore's dream. For so he dreamed. Dreamed
within a dream his own high requiem before

the English ships sailed north from Vigo,
their mastheads and their prows decked and lighted
through the night with lamps and rubies

in the story that Trafalgar tells.
Miles, Corax, Heliodromus, Pater of the bas-reliefs,
he signed the zodiac of Mithra's solstice

and hallucinated Corybantes in the skins of beasts
and flagellants where General Paget
sought to make example of deserters and had lashed

at stunted icy trees men who'd
hidden in the windowless dark huts with sick & filthy
mountaineers and who, blinded by the days

of snow, could only hear what would accompany
their punishment: a jangling
of the manacles and fetters hanging on the branded

criminals who crawled the road before them
on their hands and knees and slept
with lepers under dark façades of abbeys, while

in Bonaparte's Madrid, El Sordo painted bulls.
Bulls and bodies of the slain—
dismembered and hung up on trees like ornaments:

arms and legs, heads with genitals stuffed
in their mouths, torsos
cut off at the waist and neck and shoulders.

These the *deformis formositas ac formosa deformitas*
of the hour—torsos and toros,
packed in ice, delivered down the trails to Picasso

in a year when internationals once more decamp in Spain. . . .
Viva la Muerte's the Falangist song.
Lorca's murdered; Machado & Vallejo promptly die.

Trusting neither Mithra nor St. James, his eye
on anarchists in Barcelona,
Franco summons mercenary Moors to save the church.

VI

In the high places, they could hear the blast.
Ships rocked on the sea,
the houses at Coruña shook on their foundations

when the ammunition stores were blown.
At Santiago, bells that had burned Almanzor's oils
rang from the shock of it while men

whose job it was to ring them stood
amazed out in the square & wondered if this thunder
and the ringing was in time for Vespers

or for Nones or if it was entirely out of time.
The thunder and the ringing echoed
down the trails, back to San Millán, San Juan de la Peña,

while Maragatos looked up from their plows
and Basque shepherds among flocks near Roncevaux
turned their backs on the west & hunched

down under tall protective rocks jutting up
in frosty and transhumant fields.
Then in the high & highest places everything was still.

As it was in the beginning. Before Saint Francis
came down from the hills to Rocaforte,
before he taught his brothers how to preach & sing the word

to their little sister birds who flew into the tallest trees
and over cliffs in threefold
colored and adoring coats; before the Logos

or the Duende moved in Bertsulari singing ancient
fueros of the Basques; before Ignatius
hammered out his disciplines among the mountain rocks

breaking on the igneous of will the *ignis fatuus*
of valleys & the vagaries of love.
As it was in the beginning. . . .

                            Long before *it is*
and ever shall be under overhanging
rocks at San Juan de la Peña . . . where they say, they *say*

The Grail came to rest and made a fortress
of the monastery there carved beneath a cliff-face roof
where dowsers conjured water out of rock

in Mithra's Visigothic cave & his tauroctonous priest
drove the killing sword, like Manolete,
in the shoulder of the bellowing great beast

to burst its heart & bleed the plants & herbs across
the mountainside that monks would one day
gather there, bleed the wheat they'd make into their bread.

Everything, everything was still. As it was in the beginning
long before the silence of the abbeys,
the silence of the abbots in their solitary prayer,

the silence of the brothers cutting hay & tending sheep
at San Millán of the Cowl,
the silent sacristan measuring and pouring oils—

the weavers and the tailors and the copyists at work,
Cellarius among his stores of wool and flax,
Hortulanus in his garden tending bees—silence broken only

as Hebdomadarius, finished with the cooking, rings a bell
and even old Gonzalo de Berceo looks up happily
from silent pages where his saint has walked the mountains

in the language of Castillian *juglares* which is not,
God knows, the language of the Latin clerks. *Andaba por los montes,*
por los fuertes lugares, por las cuestas enhiestas,

but silently, and all around him it was very very still.
As it was in the beginning before silence,
in the silence that preceded silence, in the stillness

before anything was still, when nothing
made a single sound and singularity was only nothing's
song unsinging . . . aphonia

before a whisper or a breath, aphasia
before injury,
aphelion of outcry without sun . . .

                                        Long before *it is*
and ever shall be under overhanging
rocks at San Juan de la Peña, at San Millán of the Cowl,

at Loyola's Casa-Torre and the shepherds' huts
of Bertsulari in the Pyrenees
when no one spoke of *fueros* or *tristitia* or *spes,*

and there were neither rights nor hopes nor
sadnesses to speak of.
Then in the high and highest places everything was still.

As it was in the beginning. As it will be in the end.

～

Towards Pamplona, long long after all Navarre
was Spain, and after the end
of the Kingdom of Aragón, & after the end of the end,

I, John, walked with my wife Diana
down from the Somport Pass following the silence
that invited and received my song

after Europe's latest referendum. In the city of the *encierro* and
the festival of San Fermín, we drank red wines of the Ribera—Baja
Montaña, Tierra Estella—hosted by Delgado-Gomez, genius of that
place and guide Picaud. From university to citadel to bull ring,
from cathedral to the Plaza del Castillo and along the high banks
of the Arga, we walked and talked about the road to Santiago, El
Cid Campeador, Zumalacárregui and Carlist wars. For he, Delgado-
Gomez, was a native of that place. He knew the way to San Juan
de la Peña, to Leyre and Olite and Sanguessa—and so we followed
him along the river valleys, into hills, and over arid plains in the
Bardenas. And after seven days and seven nights remembering the
likes of Sancho the Wise and Sancho the Strong, the battle of Navas
de Tolosa and the chains of Miramamolín wrapped around a coat
of arms, the three of us, blest and besotted, burned by the sun but
refreshed by all the waters of the mountain streams, the shade of
many cloisters, and the breezes of the vineyards of Mañeru, crossed

the Puente la Reina ourselves, and walked that trail leading to the sea at Finisterre.

And, in the high & highest places, everything was still.

Part VII

Epilogue to a Cycle of Poems on the Pilgrim Routes to Santiago de Compostela

And this is for my daughter, who,
in the middle of the map I try to draw, the making,
struggles to a Compostela of her own

in pain & torment. *What did I do wrong?* she asks.
What did I do wrong
to suffer this?—The primal, secret, terrified & universal

query of the sick. She did nothing wrong.
And yet she walks in chains
along a Lemosina or a Tolosona Dolorosa

winding through uncertainty & grief
to disappear into unknowable remote far distances.
She walks ahead of me, doubting that

I follow, although I call out loudly & I try,
But also, when she herself must rest, unable to go on,
at hospital or hospice on the way, then

I'll learn to wait, a patient too, without impatience.
Perhaps we'll see pass by every single other living soul!
The routes were arduous, each one,

and cemeteries in the churchyards far outnumber
monuments recording cures miraculous
achieved along the way. You had to get there somehow.

You had to show the saint your poor
tormented frail human body. You had to drag it there
driven by your guilt or your desire.

The journey's so entirely strange I cannot fathom it.
And yet this map, this prayer:
That she will somehow get to Compostela,

take that how you may, & that I will be allowed to follow.
And that Santiago, call him what you like,
Son of Thunder, Good Saint Jacques, The Fisherman,

Or whoever really lies there—
hermit, heretic, shaman healer with no name—
will somehow make us whole.

After Years Away

I — MY BED, MY FATHER'S BELL

First my bed, then his, now mine again—
just for a week.

He died in it, my father, where for years
I'd lie beside my pretty love,

alive and indiscreet.
He moved in here so she, my mother,

might sleep undisturbed while he gazed darkly
all night long into the dark.

In need, he'd ring a small brass bell
molded in the shape

of a hoop-skirted lady
sweeping with a broom and looking grim.

I see it now,
lying sideways on a row of books.

He'd ring it and she'd come to him.

II — MY FATHER'S BELL, MY GRANDFATHER'S BOOKS

The books are remnants of a city gardener's
life: the works of Emerson,

a Tennyson collected, *Paradise Lost.*
He's written in his Milton

1650
1608

  42 years. And on the title page:
Begun in January, 1893, and never finished.

In another hand: *Happy new year to you, 1892.*
He's figured that J.M. was 42 in 1650

when he wrote his answer to Salmasius
and lost his sight.

Defensio pro Populo Anglicano.
At the Presbyterian funeral a cousin

asked: *are you religious?* and I said
in callow family disaffection:

Gnostic. Bogomil. Albigensian for heaven's sake.
On the *Ex Libris* plate:

Poetry. This book will not be loaned.
And underneath: *couldn't dig this month.*

Ground as cold as hell.
I replace the book. I pick up the bell.

III — MY MOTHER'S BROOM, MY FATHER'S BELL

My mother stashed those books in here
for me to find. My father

would have seen them, reaching for his bell,
but they were not for him.

She left them here, her father's only legacy,
as she began to sweep.

She swept the hearth, the porch and drive,
she even swept the street.

(She swept my father once entirely
off his feet.)

While he lay dying & while I sat reading books,
she swept his mortal breath away,

I think.
When she heard the ringing here . . .

And then swept circles round & round the bier
as I said *Gnostic, Bogomil.*

Although the ground was cold as hell
they dug the grave & dug it deep.

Sweet sleep. Sweep sweep.
There's no one here to listen or to care,

and so I ring the bell—
creating great commotion *there.*

The Key of C Does Not Know My Biography

(Stravinsky, 1937–1942)

In Sancellemoz they read the *Philokalia* while
in the rue St. Honoré his *moderato alla breve* coughed
not once for Nicodemus on Mount Athos or
Makarius of Corinth even if the resurrection were Docetic
and the tonic a familiar C.
It was the worst year of his life.
Tuberculosis drowned his daughter Mika and
his wife at Sancellemoz; he himself and then Milena
spat up blood; his mother died
and Wehrmacht panzers rumbled toward the Maginot.
He wrote in C. He wrote *Larghetto concertante*
in the sanatorium and though it was no *Sacre du Printemps*
the spring would have its rites: fists of earth
thrown in open graves at Saint Geneviève.
He wrote in C in C in C, was diatonic in extreme
and in the suite of dances the fugatos
the Italianate transparency of theme you'd never
guess he lit the candles every night in agony
beside the image of *La Vierge de perpétuel secours*.

Then Hollywood. Then the *allegreto* and the *largo*
and the Disney dinosaurs roaring to Stokowsky's *Sacre*
that frightened little children at the matinees.
Then war. Then holocaust. He wrote in C.
His one entirely boring work had saved his life
by counting repetitions like the telling of a rosary—
dominant and tonic, tonic and the dominant—
tonal bricks to build a house in which he'd pitch at last
a tall dodecaphonic tent and
call the Angel down for Abraham.
He said the key of C
did not know his biography.

That Music is the Spur to all Licentiousness

(Janáček in love)

The little birds would flutter to
his Katya's grave his Kyrie in Glagolitic
sing out lustily a *Gaspodi pomiluj.*
Salva! (Gloria!)
                    But *non credo in Signeur Dieu by god*
whispered every violin he heard
some gypsy Dorian raised fourth cantabile his word consumed &
sounding out *nápěvky* Ka-mi-la. Half his age
and twice his muse she'd be his Katya his Kabanova
his lesson to Renard & Reineke
on how to chase a fox in old Moravia. *Bystrouška!*

Still those two quartets would feed on crazy
Tolstoy fed on *Kreutzer* weeping presto by the moonlit
porch at Yasnaya Polyana: Tender Lyovochka all
undone and fucking Sonia in the nave of his own *niet*
a Pozdnychev strung out in Prague *sul ponticello.*
That music is the spur to all licentiousness
the maestro doubts. His love unconsummated he embraces
only sound. And it dissolves.
And when the Angel asks him would he
make his peace with God the dying Janáček replies
but what is peace
and what is would
and what is god Janáčková.

Received by Angels Singing Like the Birds

(*Messiaen, 1992*)

Venite . . . inginocchiatevi &
Susanna's answered
by a Garden Warbler and a Kakapo.
Figaro! Strings, cymbal, wind machine, les ondes—
those bells bells from Assisi.
L'Ange Voyageur steps from Fra Angelico's *Annunciation*
with his wings unfurled, his feathers
quinticolored red & yellow, blue & green & mauve,
and sings: *Cantico della creature cantico*
glissando Gerygone percussion tuned a new
Noh-Caledonian: *What is your name?*
Ondeolivier avec offrandes pas oubliées.
And suddenly a dawn sky of Skylarks. Orioles
and Lyrebirds, suddenly antiphony
of Icterine and Thrush. Semitone descent from A
as demisemiquaver . . . then
arpeggio of cloud,
tremolo among the shining shaken leaves.

For Kym

The Flagellant (*i.m. Percy Grainger*)

1.

Italian wouldn't do at all
to tell his band the way they ought to feel
when they played the score.

Bundle it & jogtrot through these bars, he'd say:
Lower notes of woggle well to the fore.
Easy goes but cling it, louden lots!

He'd have them lay on with a will.
He'd play the flageolet.
Some there were who'd find his ways flagitious.

2.

Melbourne in the mornings of
a mother's love:—His pregnant Rose would
gaze upon Apollo's alabaster

on her dresser, pray that he be gifted with
the sinlessness of song, and hang
the horsewhip by the empty music stand.

This son of sunlight might just winch it
short of woggle, jogtrot where he ought to cling,
bungle where the lauding rose at dawn.

3.

Carried by that praise well round the world,
Mother's "Bubbles," now her "Perks," yammered
in his made up lingo to the friends who'd listen

while he stood up naked on the lid of his piano
talking Maori Swedish German & Icelandic
all at once and lecturing the Frankfurt musicologists

on Kipling. His *Marching Song* would be performed
by whistling girls tramping through the open air
in broken strides at who/4 what/4 & in double Dutch.

4.

The *Shorter Music Dictionary* (Willi Apel, Harvard)
has no listing for *Brigg Fair*. There's no mention
there that in 1900 PG wrote a Sea Song which required

a band of winds to play at 7/35 and 9/17. Between
the *Frauenliebe* songs and *Freischütz, Der*
you won't learn anything about Free Music or the

Melanette machine or Grainger glides accomplished
by the PG System Kangaroo. *Lulu's* listed,
Lute and *Lur,* but not PG's *A Lot of Rot for Cello.*

5.

Anyhow, *Brigg Fair*. The brown wax cylinders revolved
to capture every bleat & twiddle of the lads from
Lincolnshire whose mix of Dorian Aeolian Ionian

scaled up and down the modes the way their fathers had
before the sons had left for towns and music hall.
He scored it with the jagged rhythms and the ornaments

intact. He scored it with the slides and hugged himself
with joy. He rose up in the morning with the lark
and beat himself until he bled. He broke all out in clover.

6.

And no one knew quite what *The Warriors* was.
Not Lady Elcho in her country house, the PM's mistress
and the friend of H.G. Wells; not all the Wedgwoods

or the Wedgwood-Benns; not John Singer Sargent
or his spiffy sitters or the Balfours in their motor car.
It didn't just sing *Willow Willow*, not just *Shepherd's Hey*.

Did it appeal or appall? The rich were not apprised.
While Stabat Mater nursed *le vice anglais*,
it wore out three conductors and an offstage band.

7.

If he could call himself a tone-wright & his music tonery,
he'd purge the spirochete that gnawed in Greek
and Latin at the mothertongue's profoundest roots.

He said he wasn't democratic but a-chance-for-all-y,
and he'd pound out all his tone-works
on keyed-hammer-strings. Blue-eyed English word-seeds

should replace all but the most un-do-with-outable
post-Hastings-French-begottens too. He'd oh stick-to-it-
ively drive himself to overset his thot-plan into deeds.

8.

Or go to Norway, visit Grieg. Introduce Duke Ellington
to Delius. He'd play the Green Man guising like
a geezer's dream of Morris-dancing tribes. He wore

a coat from which there dangled gewgaws & galoshes,
pencils, pens & manuscripts all tied on with
little bits of string: his only suitcase was a suite of songs.

His robin was to the greenwood gone, his Kammermusik
Strathspey in the hills. If he wasn't Grettir he'd be
Gershwin oh or Mowgli in a decorated plagal & in G.

9.

But how did one make sounds that were the sea?
In what key was a cloud? Did winds blow sharp or flat?
And when his lovers beat him with the whips

how was he to score his mother's lips?
Must he orchestrate an algolagnia for algophobes?
He'd grow all logarithmical

at loggerheads with Logos on the Loften Isles.
Blue-eyed English queried him—asked the why-grounds
for the hand-claps in the puzzle-wifty towns.

Master Class

Well, then, one more time.

Auf dem Flusse ... where you
failed to emphasize the consonants enough
and your crescendo did not swell.
Der du so lustig rauschtest ...
Liegst kalt. It's icy, understand?
What does a heartbeat sound like under ice?
Like this like this.
Let yourself be overcome by grief.

You can't? All right. Then let yourself
be overcome by joy.
Touch her and embrace her
as you did one summer on that river bank.
Unlace her bodice then. Your hand.
Right here. Heart, your heart
must break must break
because you know that she will die.

You are so young. You think these are clichés.
Your heart has never broken,
but it will. When I was young Isolde
Tristan died for me. I died for him.
You think this life is only song.
Begin again: Perhaps you favor French?
I am so old so old
and yet I do remember every touch.

So touch me. Here. Begin again, in French.
Shall you become my Pierrot Lunaire?
I'll sing for you from Berlioz:
Ma belle amie est morte.
You've never heard, I guess, of Gautier.
But if you care you'll die for me:
you'll die you'll die.
Here is the poison and the glass.

I am the mistress here, the maestro too.
This is my master class.
When you come, you'll sing it as I say.
You'll rhyme your *do*
with dildoe if I like.
You'll sing it sweetly while I play.
Der du so lustig rauschtest . . .
You'll sing it for me every day.

Diminished Third

I · EXPECTATION

The woman clad in white, large red roses
shedding petals from her dress, expects
the unexpected, wanders through a moonlit woods
where, God knows, anyone might stumble
on their lover's corpse . . .
                              Even Schoenberg
in Vienna in *Erwartung,* improvising
ostinatos, overriding bars, or Hohenzollern Isoldes
spiking Bismarck helmets at the stars—

Even Moses, who could only speak, exclaiming
Ich will singen,
counting on his finger tips the laws.

II · DOCTOR FAUST

Boxed by Thomas Mann into a magic square
with megrims, paedophiles and fictive sounds,
A.S. rages over stolen property, the rape and insult
perpetrated by this syphilitic Leverkühn who writes

a serialism no one ever heard. And yet he'd said himself
that music was a word, that language was a kind
of music too: Had in fact some rowdy losal out of hell
so pricked his blood with sophistries that nosey

novelists could smell the sulphur in his permutations?
Did *Volk* and *Führer* grow dodecaphonic in his
retrogrades, inversions; Hetaera Esmaralda somehow

ciphered in the h-e-a-e flat of it? *Sator Arepo*
tenet opera rotas. The opera would circle, right enough.
And the sower would sue for his tenet. In tenebrae.

III - THE GOLDEN CALF

Aron, was hast du getan

This Sprechstimme! This old dogmatic honky rapper
here before his time among the Angels.
He'd lecture all the Jews as all the Jews go down
all over Europe. He's safe and sound. His friend
is Mr. Gershwin and he beats the younger man
at tennis, ping pong, chess. He cannot win a Guggenheim,
cannot get performed.

Around him nothing but the idols
and the kitsch and the clichés. He's heard that in this
land of plenty no one gets a second act;
he cannot score a third and that's a fact.
Still the old Dodecaphon speaks while Aaron sings:
Ich will singen dinga dinga ding!
Anyone might stumble on a lover's corpse.

Is he Moses, Aaron, or their contradiction burning
in his brain like Leverkühn's disease?
Darf das Leid, mein Mund, dieses Bild machen?
Gershwin whistles happily: *I got plenty o' nuttin.*
Schoenberg spricht like eine glückliche hand:
Das Grenzenlose! Boundlessness!
Constellation upon constellation whirls.
Harmonielehre multiplies

by twelves through some 2000 bars and dies
with Volk and Führer.
So if the end, as Schnabel says, will justify the means,
you might as well have a nice day.
Why not keep on smiling while you
take the line of most resistance, even in LA?

A Note on Barber's *Adagio*

  . . . Back in Autumn 1963
Samuel Barber was alone and driving through
November rain in Iowa or Kansas.
When he turned on his radio he heard
them playing his *Adagio for Strings*.
Sick to death of his most famous composition,
he turned the dial through the static
until once again, and clearly—
The *Adagio for Strings*. When a third station, too,
and then a fourth, were playing it, he thought
he must be going mad. He turned off the radio
and stopped the car and got out by a fence
staring at the endless open space in front of him
where someone on a tractor plowed
on slowly in the rain . . .

The president had been assassinated
earlier that day, but Barber didn't know it yet.
He only knew that every station in America was playing
his *Adagio for Strings*.
He only knew he didn't know
why he should be responsible for such an ecstasy of grief.

For Dónal Gordon

Sadnesses: Black Seas

I

Tristia, tristia: Tomis or Constanţa
Getae or Romanian might hear . . . might go and hide
heedless of a rhetoric resounding to its own

its onerous exemplum *adynata, adynata:* Naso
whose impossibilities would rage like Dido
hurling Latin in Aeneas' wake: O Divine Augustus

bitch of an apotheosis who recoiled, call, recall
those numbers moving with a grace that no one
south of Petersburg but Alexander Pushkin

could recite that song of bodies changing
into other bodies: Mandelstam prefiguring his own
departure into darkness gaudy indigence behind

beyond the poverty of happiness: eye of Eisenstein
plotting golden sections as caesurae thinking
two & three and two & three the empty baby carriage

bumping down Odessa steps the sly and hungry
host in naval whites at Yalta grinning at the crippled
president the portly flushed personified PM:

II

Tristia, tristia: adynata, adynata:
Scythians leap up from rocks look out from trees
as cameras grind in faithless documentary

and who can tell from just that word *departure*
how long spindles hum and shuttles flutter
back and forth to measure everything that's happened

happening again but this time without either
wax or bronze: *tristia, tristia:*
all the rivers flow back up to mountain streams

the horses of old Helios stumble in their course the sea's
aflame the plow of earth cleaves heaven:
General Insov was a loyal friend but what to do

with this new Governor Voronstov good Ovidius
except go fuck his wife:
the field of honor is as boring as the gaming board:

adynata, adynata: Dr Smirnov will be shot close up
his pince-nez broken in his face if someone finds a man to play
the priest the sailors can be executed underneath a tarp

but what to do with all these little countries after such a scene
but swallow them: a ship might just as well
be named for Pushkin as Potemkin: Ovid has his statue now

and Stalin Churchill Roosevelt
it's true the birds are indiscriminate it's best no doubt
to be unknown a decent anonymity and

Mandelstam says women weave the men fall down in fields.

Persistent Elegy

*(Shortly before the 1994 South African election my former
student, Clare Stewart, was murdered in KwaZulu,
probably by an Inkatha hit squad)*

And now at last Nelson Mandela's elected.
But what of my student, Clare?
Would she have danced as she had expected?
They don't even number the dead in Rwanda.
She raises her hand in the air.
What did she do in KwaZulu to anger Inkatha?

She sits in my class long ago taking notes.
This is my student, Clare.
Volunteers have busily counted the votes.
She wakes to the voices of children.
Her daughter's among them there.
What did she do in KwaZulu to anger Inkatha?

No volunteers can describe what nobody sees.
She leaves a note in the mission.
She walks by the lake, the flowering trees.
Observers say the election is fair.
She gets in a pick-up, drives from the village.
She raises her hand in the air.

She tries to answer the question.
What did you do in KwaZulu to anger Inkatha?
What is the answer, Clare?
They don't even number the dead in Rwanda.
Nobody's counting there.
But what did she do in KwaZulu to anger Inkatha?

She raises her hand in the air.
And now at last Nelson Mandela's elected.
What of my student, Clare?
She never arrives where she is expected.
Everyone's weeping there.
What did she do in KwaZulu to anger Inkatha?

What of my student, what of my student, Clare?

My Mother's Webster

She'd never tell me how to spell a word;
Go look it up, she'd say. She'd say *It's there in Webster,*
pointing to the battered blue and dog-eared dictionary
that she'd lugged from Georgetown to Columbus long
before those Anglo-Saxon expletives she said offended her
entered the American Heritage. I find it at the bottom of a box
unpacking things I thought to save when she turned vague,

lost the words she'd loved, and started groping for a few
remembered monosyllables to get her through a day of
meals, treatments, therapies, and baths at Olentangy Home.
Her house is sold; she's 92; and I decide to look it up
when I'm unsure about how one spells *Houyhnhnm*
and want to write a footnote citing Swift in *Gulliver.*
The facing page is black with marginalia; it's in her hand.

What alchemy is this? *A curse on Sally Smothers*
she has written, circled, arrowed to *hostility*
in one direction, *hothead* in another. *Turn the page*
she writes, and there beside the underlined *horned toad*
and *hornet* she abbreviates, *S.S.,* with arrows to *horrendous.*
She writes: *My friends: Eleanor, Elizabeth, and Jean.*
She writes: *The boy I do not love: Jason Dean: ZZ.*

Some words are simply canceled: *housewife* with an X,
hooker with a line; the illustrations under *horseshoe*
toss her up to *horah,* ring her to *hosanna; horn of plenty* is
a *cornucopia,* and that is circled six or seven times.
Next to *horologe* she writes *ding-ding* and clearly likes
hornswoggle, prints in little caps: *They'll do it every time.*
She writes *I'll host a hostage in the hostel, my hors d'oeuvre!*

Who is this language sprite? It seems to be my mother
talking to herself in 1917. There's still heavy fighting on
the western front; her father has just died; she'll meet *my* father
in another seven years. There is no sulfa yet, no penicillin;
Eleanor and Jean will get the post-war flu and not survive.
I've never heard her mention Jason Dean. She will, in fact,
become a housewife and she'll outlive Sally Smothers

that old hothead she called *hornet* and *horned toad*.
The goddesses of seasons, Horae, might have taught her
in good time a ripe Horatian patience as she gazed
at *horoscope* and then *horizon*—looked up from the page
and out her bedroom window at the *horos*, boundary,
tangent plane across the surface of the globe defining
the conjunction of the earth and sky. She writes:

I guess that means about as far as I can see.
There's not a mark here or an indication that she saw her
future linked to *hospital* or *hospice*—
nor to *Houyhnhnms*, rational and gentle creatures
one might like for neighbors even at the Olentangy Home
and whose name I cannot spell. I can hear her say again
Well go and look it up, It's there in Webster,

meaning this particular blue book, and not some other.
I'd look her up herself if I could find her. She's always in,
but she is never there. She's here in 1917 and not hornswoggled
or intimidated or a hostage in some hostel where they
do it every time. There's a horseshoe on her door.
There's not a single cloud on the horizon and it's June.
She'll be her own hors d'oeuvre and dance the horah round

a horn of plenty. She writes: *I'm Thirteen in Three Days.*

The Singing

Now we could talk. Too late,
too long ago I see you
in that chair and see
myself unwilling and impatient

and so full of hurry that I
hurt to get away and say
some quick and careless thing
which turns out to be all

I managed as the final words
I spoke to you. But now,
now we could talk. I have grown
patient. I sit as you once sat

alone most days and stare at nothing.
I know—too late, too well—what
you might say, or rather might have said,
what I will never now respond to you

but only mutter to myself or into darkness.
It sounds like sorrow. I mean the sound
of it is sorrow as some kind of song.
It's not so much a saying, then, as singing?

Did you want to sing to me that day
some twenty years ago, for me to sing to you?
Dear God what kind of song? What sorrow
sings what wretchedness to bed?

You did not go to bed. You sat. Your heart.
More rest from sitting up all night
than lying down. And all night long you sang.
Sang only to yourself because

there's no one ever who will listen
to such song. I know. I sing.
We'd sing that song together if you
were alive—the only one you sang,

the only one I sing beneath what talk
I can what tense I cannot manage
knowing far too late too well how long
you sat in what was never silence

what was never anything but song.
Now we could talk. Now we'd keep our silence
perfectly and hear each other sing.
Your past my future in that present when

impatient I heard nothing and went out.

Left Hands and Wittgensteins

For Roy Fisher at Seventy and, inter alios, Leon Fleisher, Blaise Cendrars

Paul's brother Ludwig the philosopher had said
the world is everything that is the case
in case you lost your arm. In case you could not play
for all the world. *No left hand*
we used to say as glib precocious critics of the young
Ahmad Jamal, one of us the southpaw pitcher
on the high school baseball team who struck out every
righthand batter in the junior league.
But Paul was *all* left hand who bitched at both Ravel
and Sergei Prokofiev but nonetheless
performed their music no right hand would ever play.
The world was everything that was the case
when Blaise Cendrars also lost his arm. In that same war.
In that same war where everything that was the case
exploded in the world. My friend the southpaw pitcher studied
in the end with Leon Fleisher who awoke one day
with no right hand as a result of carpal-tunnel stress. A syn-
drome: drone, his repertory was diminished but he played
Prokofiev he played Ravel, and all thanks due to Wittgenstein
whose world was everything that was the case.

Left hand, left wing? Roy, are all right-handers Tories
in their bones? They'd case your joint as if
they'd lost most everything left in the world.
(Or would you pack them in your case with all the world
except for B and exit in that key?) I weep
for your right arm, your stroked-out days of therapy,
your egging on your brain to find a few more millimeters
of its limb. But what's permission but commission
to a left-hand poet, left-hand pianist at seventy?
You might well go ask Wittgenstein, might well ask Cendrars.
Then go ahead—put the piano at risk, put the poem
in jeopardy: Millennium's a comin' after, Roy:

If anything could be the case
the world is everything that is the case.
Are those iambs, da-dah da-dah? Is that in 4/4 time?

Geneva Pension

Once a year my wife's mother, Mrs. Adams, 93,
receives in her mail at Farnam, Surrey,
a letter from Geneva asking, in effect,
are you still alive? It comes along with her

League of Nations pension, still paid
to her as the widow of a naval attaché.
She laughs and says: *I guess we are not many.*
Out of curiosity, she once wrote back

and asked: *How many are we, in fact?*
A polite letter came a few weeks later
in which an official—one wonders just what kind—
had written at the end, *In fact, six.*

By the time it reached the secretary to be typed
evidently things had changed: she or he had lined out "six"
and just above it written "five."
But indeed Captain Adams was a League of Nations

officer in residence. There they were, a veteran
of the World War and his so much younger wife.
Their high hopes faded like a sunset
on the lake. Or like the hopes of a tall hieratic

figure they would see standing with a walking stick
beside the lake and evidently talking to
himself: O.V. de L. Milosz, metaphysician, French poet,
citizen of Lithuania. "Will the hour be new

in some archaic future?" Milosz asked before
the war. *Nouvelle, mais si peu neuve* . . .
By 1922 he heard an insect's cry within him,
underneath the ashes of his heart . . .

Thinking in French or Polish or maybe even German,
he stood there by the lake and, in a highly formal way,
inclined his head politely to the English Captain
and his wife as they passed him on their promenade.

There in Surrey, early June, Mrs. Adams looks a little
quizzically at the check, then at the picture of
her husband leaning on the window sill in
morning sun. Elsewhere, four other widows of the League

receive Geneva pensions and may also greet the day.

Reception

When the tired old poet's genuine modesty
and quiet life in the small university town
had finally made him all but invisible in the larger
world of literature, his former friend arrived

out of the past for a visit between readings
and appearances on television talk shows.
When the old poet's wife thought she heard
the condescension in the faint praise

the famous writer offered of what would be
her husband's final book, she took him aside
to fill up his wine glass and quietly said
You know, Ernest's poems have always been

better than yours, which are full of
bombast and pretension. Although I wasn't
meant to hear that, I did. Remembering it now,
I also think of Ernie telling me one night

about the way Eileen, young and pretty then
and not just some professor's wife,
used to dance like Carmen on the tables
of a local Polish bar . . .

Unfinished

I - HAYDN

    . . . just those lines by Gleim,
Der Greis a part song now divided
among parts for voiceless strings that
whispered wordlessly *Hin ist alle meine*
Kraft, alt und schwach bin ich . . .
His strength . . . and all his skill . . .
Also printed on a card the servant gave
to those who'd come around & ask
for more. No more. No strength. No craft.
He'd hole-up like some crofter mumbling
I am old and weak. Two movements
in D minor of the last quartet just stop at
Menuetto ma non troppo Presto.
Then the four-part setting of the fifty
silent words that ended *Ein harmonischer*
Gesang . . . mein Lebenslauf

II - SCHUBERT

The B Minor torso not unveiled, of course,
until December 1865. By then, all his friends
had also died. Two years earlier, sections
of his *Lazarus* cantata were performed. He had in fact
emerged quite often from his tomb, and while one
critic spoke in wonder of his "posthumous diligence"
another warned against "the adulation of
his relics." Endless bits and pieces and a range
in scale: a tenth symphony, the opera called
Der Graf von Gleichen, tossed-off riffs

of uncompleted lied, sketches for a symphony in D,
Adrast and *Sakuntala*, *Quartettsatz*,
a piano sonata in C, endless spare or
missing parts. You could construct with some
of these a Schubert of your own, and many
people tried. Was it protofascist Metternich Vienna
at his throat that made his doppelganger
sing the Agnus Dei of the E-flat mass?
The Karlsbad Degrees and Count Sedlnitzky
drove his good friend Johann Senn
to exile and arrested his own work. His illness
did the rest. Charged with an "opprobrium of language,"
his optative became oracular in Heine, but his
doppelganger sang the Agnus Dei of the E-flat mass.

III - Shostakovich

... and why not
give the opus number of that Gogol opera
left behind in Leningrad to Stalin's
NKVD choristers for song and dance,
Otchizna obbligati very much obliged?
For unacknowledged legislators, 63 might
suit the People's Commissariat to an ironic t.
A little joke on uncle Joe's police
from the abandoned *Gamblers*, scoundrel
fragments only sung out posthumously
three years after the sonata for viola
which had quoted them. Quoted them
in what became his actual farewell—omissions long
admitted in commissions from the state—

to Leningrad & Moscow & in fact not least
to Gogol's ghost still singing Gavryushka's song
about the better life in Ryazan and haunting
through a nearly empty Gulag

The Lyric Suite: Aldeburgh Festival, Snape

Consummate in sound, *appassionato,*
Alban Berg's unconsummated love for Werfel's sister!
Her initials, H and F, conjoined with his own
as in a page illuminated in the mind
from *Kells* or Lindisfarne, locked to Schoenberg's mathematics.
Hanna's copy of the score alone
sang the unsung text, penciled in and set
but then erased. The quote from *Tristan.*
Then the *De Profundis Clamavi* of Baudelaire.

How alien this passion sounds arching out of Hanna's Prague
of 1925 and into evening mists of a tranquil Suffolk summer,
weaving through the reeds around the Alde
and reaching on towards Orford church to dissipate
like unfulfilled desire.
And yet how I desire you, listening and failing
to listen to this sound, drifting
on a music of my own, then returned abruptly to this hall
by stricture and precision.

Allegretto gioviale . . . and the theme,
the twelve-tone row, enclosed by her initials.
"No hint," he wrote, "of tragedy to come."
Near us here, the old mill at Letheringham
is still. The wheel turned the year they wrote
the Doomsday Book. I've known this landscape
now for twenty years, felt it utterly
suffused with the presence of the woman here
beside me. Heavy rain this morning
sent the peahens scurrying, a huddle of ducks
and guinea fowl disappearing among reeds.
Daffodils were thick along the stream.
A tree trunk full of moss. Small brick cottage,

dull red tiles on its roof. . . . I sit
beside the woman I have loved for twenty years.
I think of someone else.

I think of you, and I desire you, listening
and failing to listen to this sound,
as he desired you himself, straining for the boundary
of expression as the spindle of his time unwound,
listening and failing to listen
to the voices of Vienna, generations of them
singing in a thousand violins, all those
strings attached to every note he wrote, every string
played pizzicato saying *du du du*
and meaning *her,* and yet he too desired you,
wrote his program into what I hear
and do not hear, writing letters with his other hand
to say *I was unfaithful to you only during*
a performance of the Mahler, only
because Mahler took my mind from you, my love,
but only for an hour, thinking really *Hanna, Hanna,*
whom he called Mopinka, and his program,
amoroso, then *misterioso* and *ecstatico.* . . .

And why should not your name be Hanna? since
I cannot name you? since you have today no other name?
since I think of you as *thou* but need to call
out now, to call out and to whisper both, to call
you by some name, to whisper in the silence between
movements *Do you hear the singing now?* to be assured
that no one does, and not to mean do you,
do *you* hear it who are part of it as word and sound,
nor in any way confuse you with my love,
my love, linking your initials in some page

illuminated in the mind from *Kells* or Lindisfarne—
Hanna, then, Mopinka.

Do you hear the singing now? But now there is no singing,
was no singing but for those who heard it
in imagination, two of them and two of us . . .
She shakes her head, and in the space between
the *presto delirando* and the *largo*
landscape opens from the hall beside the Alde
and into time. A secret name, and an acknowledged name,
inhabit it. And are there always two?
The mill stream at Letheringham flows beneath
the wheel, the Alde by Snape and Iken,
then below the Orford castle keep and to the sea.
Water fowl leave their hieroglyphic prints
on mud as slick as oil while the tidal river shrinks
into a ribbon and the boats lie crazily
at angles in the ooze and weeds. Darkness comes
to Tunstall Forest, Campsea Ash and Woodbridge.
Again the quartet plays, *desolato* now.

My cry arises from a landscape with no brook
or tree, no field or flock, where air is lead and where
in shadows terror looms . . . As if some tenor
might emerge from such a place and stretch his voice
four octaves on the rack of *Fleurs du Mal* . . .
The cold terror of this icy star . . . *and of this*
night . . . *So slowly does*
the spindle of our time unwind . . . When all is done
we do what is expected, clap our hands
and shuffle up the isle while four musicians,
after bows, pack up instruments and leave the quiet hall.
Berg's Helene listened to this suite one summer night

some sixty years ago. Who knows what she heard?
She spoke of neither fear nor of desire.
When all was done, she did what was expected,
clapped her hands and shuffled
up the aisle while the four musicians,
after bows, packed up instruments and left the quiet hall,
so slowly did the spindle of their time unwind.

And now the landscapes cease
to alternate, to overlap: Prague returns to Prague,
Vienna to Vienna, and I am here in Suffolk by the Alde.
I walk away in moonlight like some dizzy Pierrot,
some Pierrot Lunaire. . . .
Beside me there is just one woman,
steady and serene—
and silent as the silent endless last indifferent sky.

Black Dog

The black dog's in the room with us
and yet we joke about his bark.
He's bitten Joe. He's bitten me.
At the moment, he's asleep. We'd rather
have a large indifferent cat beside the hearth,
but somehow this black dog came in again
who's all too keen to get involved.
He ate the dinner that we couldn't eat ourselves.
He picked his teeth with our pencils.
We'd like to write him off, but he's
written *Canine* on our poems. He doesn't
get our jokes and we can't just get up
and go. We'd talk about our travels
but this isn't Argos sleeping here.
We're left with what he'll let us do,
which isn't much: We'll only speak of him
until he hears the wolf-calls in the night &
wakes up from his dream of our confinement.

for Joe Francis Doerr

Ohio Forebears

ALBERT C.

He'd vaccinate at gun point if he had to
when there was an epidemic. Out he'd go
in what his son still called a "buggy"
in the 1940s. Friendly with the gun strapped

on his hip, he'd had it since a rebel
shot him through the elbow in the Civil War.
Eventually, he lost the arm, but not
before he used both hands delivering

uncounted babies in Gilboa and McComb.
Born on the battle's anniversary, his son
was given "Shiloh" as a middle name.
With 10,000 dead on either side, who would

light the candles on his cake? Beauregard retreated.
Pittsburgh Landing held. But the dark
in the covenant was truly arked.
Albert kept his arm in a bottle of formaldehyde

underneath a cupboard by the coal chute.
Now and then he'd go and have
a look at it. The gun was given in his will
to Edward Shiloh and the arm

was buried with him when he died.

Edward Shiloh

The gun was quite antique in '98, but
he took it with him anyway. No Rough Rider,
he nonetheless claimed Teddy R as his
own man and spoke with jingo confidence.

Although he never got to Cuba, Supreme Court
pages said they'd seen him in his uniform
that hangs in tatters in my closet by
the judge's robe that he and then my father wore.

He was distinguished for the wisdom and the style
of his opinions which are studied even now
in schools of law. He'd pace the upstairs study floor
incanting: *Goddamn the goddamn damn.*

My father said to him one night: *I wish you'd taught
me how to curse.* His bookshelves bulged
not only with The Law, but poetry:
With Kipling & with Whitman & with Tennyson . . .

At ten I sat there on his floor with Gunga Din.
I loved each button on his uniform, his
epaulettes, the dull dress sword. But most of all
the pistol brought from Shiloh with a shattered arm.

A large bronze bust they made of him
and put it in the State House where for fifty years
he was Ohio's Justice Holmes. The plaster cast,
intact for many months, shattered into pieces

in the hallway where it stood beside our phone.
A call from someone with bad news—
all about the trouble I'd got into at my school—
and suddenly the patriarch was dust.

The papers said he'd slipped and fallen
from a window where he tried to show exterminators
where the squirrels got into the house. But I knew
this synchronicity was all my fault. Although the bronze

statue stood upon its pedestal, I knew
that phone call somehow broke the plaster cast and
pitched him out the window, too. I believed in the uncanny:
Pittsburgh Landing calling yet to Shiloh & to Beauregard,

the finger on a severed arm pointing straight at me.

JOHN MARSHALL

It's hard to be a judge and named for Marshall
but at least he wasn't monikered
for some battle in the Spanish War. The family
used to sing the bully anthems and they all

remembered the Maine. He missed the war his
own generation fought because rheumatic fever
licked his heart with flame and made him, unlike
Albert C and Edward S, unfit to serve.

His ill health followed him in ways I never knew
until he died. What he wanted was to serve.
The state. His family. Something, anyway.
When Edward Shiloh fell out of that window

and I thought my truancies from school had been
the cause, he won the unexpired term
and wore his father's robe as if it were a uniform.
And that was what destroyed him.

He was a shy and rather simple man and what
he could do well he did before
he had to live up to his name. His level
was Municipal, and traffic court his calling.

Although they made no bust of him, they cast
his name in bronze and screwed it
to his office door. It might as well have said:
Give up hope all Ye who enter here.

He entered every day. A hundred yards away
his father's statue stood.
He stuck it out for something like a dozen years
and then resigned, humiliated by his frailty.

JOHN EDWARD

Ohio forebears on a shelf imported from
all over: Pooh and Rupert,
Paddington and Roosevelt, Delmore Schwartz.
And books to tell their tales.

Even Pooh's is sad, abandoned in the end
by the boy he loved and served.
As for me, I guess I'm Albert's severed arm,
I'm Edward Shiloh's plaster cast,

John Marshall's dickey heart, the clumsy foot
of Paddington at tea time—
a badly broken covenant with all
of them and exiled in a place

I thought I chose that isn't Rome or Tomis
either one but closes borders on your
marches where the cars are stalled and all
the horses sleeping in their harnesses

& Sherman's not recruiting any more, Ohio.

Variations on the Song of Songs

For Laura and Elliot

What shall a father say to his daughter, the bride?
The beams of our house were of cedar.
The rafters were branches of fir.

And then to the bridegroom, what can he say?
This woman you love once was a laughing child.
The beams of her house were of cedar.

And as she grew up she also grew down—
Down into the center of things,
and up where the beams were of cedar—

and there in her house she grew wise, though at first
nobody noticed, for she was a laughing child
and her rafters were branches of fir.

But the cedar and fir came from a song,
the rafters and beams were all singing:
And out of the song came a bridegroom who said:

What shall a man say to this woman, his bride?
May the beams of our house be of cedar,
our rafters the branches of fir,

May we sing out *Shir ha-Sharim*
For this daughter and son, this woman and man:
May we celebrate with this song:

Rafter and beam, Song of all Songs, *Shir ha-Sharim*.

Letter to an Unborn Grandson

For Ian Joshua, Laura & Elliot

Ian Joshua!—for that will be your name—
    I've written many poems
        as elegies to people who have died,

but haven't yet addressed one
    to a person not quite with us yet.
        I'm so slow at writing poems these days

you may well have been born
    before I'm finished,
        but my intention is to have this

in your mother's hands at least a week before
    your scheduled birth.
        I need to tell you this and that about

its form and why I've chosen it.
    William Carlos Williams, a doctor
        who was also one of our best poets,

thought the three line stanzas
    that he started writing late in life
        had finally captured the American idiom

he'd sought in all his writing
    in what he came to call a "variable foot."
        I've studied it a bit and have to tell you

that in fact I can't quite figure out
    what he meant
        & don't know if he really knew himself

in any kind of analytic way.
  But it doesn't really matter since the fact remains
    that he wrote these poems

that move a little bit
  like this
    in stepped down three-ply lines

late in life and deep in illness
  which have moved me off and on
    for many years. I've always loved

the great poems of the old—by men like
  Yeats and Hardy,
    men like my old friend Sandeen,

a poet whom your mother knew
  when she was young
    and used to visit mainly for the excellent

desserts his wife prepared—Eileen,
  in Ernie's life a counterpart of Williams'
    Floss, to whom he

wrote the best of all his later poems, whose love & care
  kept him going once his
    health began to fail. Now that I am

growing old myself, I read these poets even
  more, seeking to discover
    what the next thing is that life has got in store

for me. It's oddly not unlike when I was adolescent
        and read erotic work
                to learn about the mysteries of sex that

I anticipated with such eagerness. We didn't have
        explicit movies then or porn-
                ographic magazines, but D.H. Lawrence,

Henry Miller, and Anais Nin did fine.
        The old poets
                also wrote erotic poems when they

were young, and that's perhaps the reason
        they could write so well
                about the dark and final death that

followed all the little deaths from
        which one got right
                up & out of bed & put one's pants

back on, and went about one's
        daily work. It may seem odd to write to you
                at your age about sex,

but, Ian Joshua, that's the reason
        you got where you are
                right now. Because of that and love.

And there's another reason
        that I'm writing to you in this form.
                When your mother

started getting quite impatient to be born
        we went off quickly
                to the local hospital. It wasn't far, just

two blocks away. I grabbed a book
        to take along which
                happened to be William Carlos Williams'

all but posthumous last book.
        In those days older male obstetricians
                still liked fathers

out of sight for a delivery,
        and so I sat with other nervous men, reading
                Williams, waiting for your mother

to be born. I had reached page sixty-three,
        "The Turtle," when
                a nurse came in and asked me if I'd

like to see my daughter.
        And there your mother was—
                looking wide-eyed at the world

and making a terrific row. I stared at her amazed
        and wrote down in the margin
                of the Williams book "*Laura born,*

October 23 at 9:04 p.m., right in the
        middle of this poem."
                There's more. "The Turtle" has a dedication:

For My Grandson. He'd commissioned, evidently,
from his grandfather a poem
about a turtle, the grandson's only pet,

and Williams wrote it happily. *Upon his back,*
he said, *shall ride*
to his conquests, my Lord, you!

He is all wise
and can outrun the hare.
Williams by that time could hardly

walk, could barely type, sometimes
couldn't even speak
so that family & his friends & all

the many poets who admired him
could understand what he meant.
But he went on writing poems,

sometimes feeling guilty for
the time he'd spent among the avant-guardists
of New York

when he should have been with patients
back in Rutherford.
I can easily imagine now his gentle hands

upon your mother's belly,
his stethoscope listening to your heartbeat.
He had delivered hundreds and

hundreds of babies in his day,
  one of them the Rutherford policeman
    who led off the procession

to the cemetery where they buried him.
  Stroke after stroke
    he grew more feeble, poem after poem

he thought might be his last. "The Turtle"
  came quite late.
    Ian Joshua! It's hard to be a poet; don't

go down that path
  unless you've got a lifeline
    to the practicalities of living like

this doctor did; it's a risky business
  and it makes you an observer
    even of your own observations.

It makes you peek and pry;
  even he invaded privacies
    like I'm invading yours right now

before you're even born!
  Some free advice: Love your mother
    who will love you very much even

when you don't believe she does.
  Love your father equally.
    And when you grow as they say "up"

find some good that you can do
　　with work however difficult
　　　　that brings you joy & brings nobody harm.

When Williams praised the calling of the poet
　　— and he often did —
　　　　and said "I am a poet, I am!"

and when he praised Imagination and its forms,
　　I think he must have known
　　　　that it was all those souls that he had

helped into the world, bright new lives
　　like yours about to start
　　　　that in the end redeemed both him and everything

he wrote. And so to each a turtle:
　　To you, your mother, and your dad. From me,
　　　　this scribbling in the margin of a doctor's book.

Swell

For Diana

I

The lake was swell that year. The fishing too
was swell both there and in the rivers, but especially swell
was that one lovely girl among the group from
Horton Bay. It was 1920 and he'd lived
somehow through shelling at Fossalta di Piave that
he'd write about, and then escaped the influenza
which had killed more people than the war itself,
among them Edward, eldest son of my own
Grandfather M, himself a veteran of the Spanish War
and Spanish flu . . .
                    In 1950 there I am
with my one fish, a bass. I caught it trolling from a boat
in Walloon Lake and someone took my picture
holding it up high. That's the full extent of my experience
and success as angler. But it was swell that day.
I was ten and I'd been on the lake since dawn.
They all say things are swell in early Hemingway.
We say things are great, even when they're not, even
when they're only fair-to-middling, even when
they're only average to a fault. Great time. Great lake.
Great girl. Those things that were swell.
We say it sometimes with a lean sarcastic sneer
and sometimes really mean it.

Two or three years later I began to read him.
I thought he was just great. Who didn't in those days
before they wrote his life, counted up his whiskies and his pills,
and told his secrets as he went to seed somewhere out in Idaho
and at the Mayo Clinic where they gave him so much
ECT he thought his house in Cuba was in Kenya
and his second wife his first, his third some kind of matador.

I read about Nick Adams on the lake and all those
summer people first at Horton Bay and then in Paris and
Pamplona. They all said swell and I thought they were great
and even read the prose aloud. The names of places
that I knew myself would make me dizzy with the recognition
as I whisperingly incanted them in bed where I was often ill:
Petoskey, Charlevoix, Boyne Falls . . .

If I knew these I might know Paris too
and even some swell girl who'd maybe show me her swell cunt,
a word that Scribners didn't let him print but that I knew anyway
from dirty-talking Nell on Hudson Street. We'd summer up in
Michigan on Walloon Lake like he did. At Shadow Trails Inn. I loved
my father then the way he had loved his, who taught
him how to fish and hunt before he lost his mind
and put a bullet in his brain. I think my father took the picture.
There I am holding up my bass.

II

It's now 2000 and we can't find Windemere. Thirty years
between his final summer here and 1950; fifty years
between my one big catch and this boat on the lake without a line.
Things have not been swell, have not been great.
Well, sometimes they were swell: a while ago, & in another country.
His phrases stuck forever in your mind provided that
you read him very young.

But this week is okay. We've taken walks,
eaten whitefish both at Pippin's and the Walloon Inn,
and tried to figure what it means at sixty still to be alive.
Who at ten or twenty sees himself in forty, fifty years?

Robert Lowell barely made it; Berryman,
who sat cross-legged in my Salt Lake City room
and recited every word verbatim of *A Clean, Well-Lighted Place*
only got to fifty-eight. He said that story was a poem, and
he was right. I'm older than my teacher was
when he died. I'm older than Lowell. About the age
when Hemingway, who, like his father, like crazy Mr. B,
knew he'd had enough.

                    I haven't had enough.
I'm greedy and want more. I like it here on this swell lake
and looking at the shoreline passing by like print
you scan searching for that great passage you can't find
but once had known by heart. The one that either
let you through into some other world or knocked you dead.

To read at all when I first read meant simply to read him.
Misogynist or drunk, vain & boastful & commercially
successful ruin like they say, he gave me passage anyway
to pass on by, forgetting & ungrateful. Now I have no interest
in those other houses on the shore, even in what's left of
Shadow Trails Inn, which all at once I locate from a bright
configuration of some oddly angling birches
that I haven't seen for fifty years. When we were here before
I didn't know about his cottage. Windemere.
He couldn't find it either until Paris when he'd lost it
in his life to win it for his art.
And then began to say that certain things were swell:
a lake, a girl, a morning catch of trout.
A clean well-lighted place was only clean and bright.

There's yet another photograph of everyone
at Shadow Trails Inn. Everyone but me, so this time

I was the photographer. Not a single person there was left alive.
Dick and Mary, John and Lois, Jim and Florence,
Cousin Nancy, Uncle Bob—there they were against a wall,
the flag up flapping on the pole. Some firing squad
from *In Our Time* must have come and shot them where they stood,
and there was nothing I or anyone could do.
It must have happened as I turned and looked away.

III

        Just how old
was Nico A. when he walked all dazed & drawn through Italy,
when he finally laid that girl in Horton Bay
having slain the others anyway with rugged looks and laughter.
(Lots of irresistible bad rhymes with Hemingway.)
My wife was Adams too (Diana) when we met in 1966.
She was swell & great & it was London & in May.

She points at something from the bow. A scene straight
out of *Gatsby* in a stately choreography
on someone's lawn. The swells are dressed in morning suits,
although it's afternoon, and pastel-colored gowns, tinkling ice cubes
in their glasses waiting for the host and hostess
circulating on the terrace, pitchers in both hands, to pour another Pims.
The rich are different from the rest of us, said Scott.
They have bigger boats. Ours is maybe fifteen feet, plus outboard.
In a larger craft than this, I did in fact reach Paris.
Reached Pamplona, too. It's taken me a lifetime to prefer it here.
When I met Diana at some crazy Sixties party
she was standing at the far end of a narrow room and
looking like an advert for the mini-skirt. Was she
the cover-girl of that month's issue of *Time Out*

that featured "The Most Stunning Birds in London"?
(Birds of course were women who were swell.)
Men would stop & stare at her in the street. One man
wrecked his car, craning for a better look.
I couldn't believe my luck. And now she points again:
at naked swimmers in the lake, breast and buttock visible
with each new stroke, heading
from that Daisy of a dock across the lake to Eagle Point.

I like the old man's late erotic work. The things he couldn't
publish and kept working on in spite of hopeless odds
against completing them. Scribners held *The Garden of Eden*
for decades. How he loved the way those three, those
two birds and the guy, try things out he now could never do.
And even Nick and Littless seem intent on incest as they
light out for the territory half a mile from here while Mr. Packard
at the shop detains the wardens blathering about tobacco.
Left unfinished, Nick's last story stops at *Sure* when Littless
asks *And will you read it? Or is it too old to read out loud?*
Too old to read out loud? She's brought along *Wuthering Heights.*
Or did she mean Am *I* too old to ask you for this gift?
He'll read to her. It's swell, and so is she. She cuts her hair
like Catherine on the Cote d'Azur, calls herself a boy.
She says that they'll have children, swings her child's legs
astraddle on his hips. Sure, he says, I'll read.

He stops it there. His friend E.P. got back to Italy because
the rich old novelist could write him a swell check.
E.P.: who said to Lowell he'd started with a swollen head
to end with swollen feet. Hem, who measured Scott's
small cock & told him, Look: it only counts engorged with blood.

IV

The bodies of the dead lay all around him, drained
of blood, all engorged with gangrenous corruption. He thought
he'd lose his leg, and by the time he knew he wouldn't
was in love. The story is well known.
The facts as he reported them from time to time are questioned,
but the story is well known. It was Red Cross for sure
and not Italian infantry in which he served, but what the hell.
Some of what he said he did he didn't really do.
But he was born to tell a tale or two. They dug the shrapnel
from his leg and tore apart his knee to reassemble it.
He thought one night he felt his soul ascend out of his body
and return. His lady married, in the end, somebody else;
He came back here to heal . . .
                                        We stopped in Horton Bay
to buy a paper at the general store. It seems to be
unchanged. The BBC had once brought in a film crew for a shoot
and asked the puzzled clerk: *Can we buy these?*
Presenting him a shopping list preserved for eighty years
scribbled out by Mrs. H, the doctor's wife.
They still sold everything except some kind of ghastly Spam.
Embarrassed that we only had a paper, I also
bought a bottle of Chablis. We've got it with us in the boat.
Was that the store where Mr. Packard had detained the wardens
letting Nick and Littless make their run?

The man next door at Red Fox Inn would know. He'll sell you
books or cook your lunch or put you up at night.
He's got the place declared a National Historic Site, and tells you
this is "Fox's House" in "Up in Michigan." Tempted
by a copy of 3 *Stories* & 10 *Poems* which I had never seen, I
noticed it was Xeroxed in between the warping boards

he'd stitched and glued himself. He knew the canon like a Priest
his Bible, but he hadn't read or didn't like much else. . .
Mr. Faulkner? No. Mr. Fitz? A friend of Hem's. Mr. Joyce?
You mean that irksome Irishman? He'd made some maps with
marks and annotations noting where each incident occurred in all
the stories and he gave us free gummed labels saying
*purchased from the heir of Volie Fox, fishing guru who taught
Hemingway his tricks.* We stuck one on the bottle of Chablis.

He had my number, though, and shouted out *Goodbye Professor!*
and I turned about to say, *well actually I don't teach Him,*
but only waved, and thought of one old Brother in the Art, fired both
by and for his genius at my place of work, teaching even
Across the River to his Freshmen, saying of poor Cantwell,
If he could well he would well but he can't well.
The students, still too young to get it, laughed politely, none
of them as yet with serious wounds.
My friend was early wounded though he'd not been in a war.
He too left his shit and fluids in a hole he'd
dug in lethal earth which had not blessed him for his works.

V

Well, the perks of academia. That's why you are here
says my antagonist, some voice internalized
of Mr. Volie Fox. It's called a leave. It's a sabbatical.
Get off my gown. I'll gouge your eye out
with the corner of my mortarboard.
You're corrupt as all the rest, says Volie Fox,
even though you don't talk theory and you evidently
like to read. But you can't fish.
What you really go for is what Packard at his general store
tells his wife he hates: Chautauquas. You like culture.
You'd rather go to them than to revivals where
at least they get worked up and fuck each other afterwards.
Packard liked young Nick because he saw him swelling up
with original sin. This fishing boat's a kind of
water-slumming and you can't spend half an hour
on the lake without a book & wine . . .

And yet the water sometimes blesses even lubbers
and their books. The swells of southern seas, rivers, lakes, fjords
and even damned up creeks like one I played in near my house
on Old Glen Echo Drive. All water's amniotic, nowhere Lethe,
and we watch with joy those naked girls swimming
there some fifty yards in front of us like two fine porpoises before
a ship that's making for a landfall. On land you do fall down,
so any fool builds his house or city near the ocean,
or the river or the lake. Even bourgeois mother's sons from
Oak Park Illinois were close enough to smell
Lake Michigan in western winds and bend to its bravado.
Colonel Cantwell sans Viagra lay beside his girl
in Venice; in that gondola he knew she was the angel of death,
but rocked with her on the canal. And at the start

young Nick, whose lover called him Wemedge, heard
along with waves that lapped on shingle there at Horton Bay,
I love it, Wemedge. Love it. Wemedge, come.

Chautauquas came with Methodists & Women's Christian Temperance
to Petosky, where also Sherwood Anderson had lost his
scalp, burlesqued in *Torrents of Spring*. Packard who dislikes
Chautauquas also rails against "resorters," "change-of-lifers"
sitting on hotel front porches in their rocking chairs.
He must have been a friend of Volie Fox.
His wife on culture: "Packard, I won't bother you with this,
but it really makes me feel swell."
And on her change-of-life: "I'm still all the woman you can handle,
aren't I now" . . .
               We cut the outboard at the sand bar
and we open the Chablis. Still no sign of Windemere
that we can see. Diana points again. Unembarrassed, tall and brazen,
both the naked girls walk up on the sandy beach
and shake the water off their golden bodies like two dogs.
Then they turn to us and smile.

    VI

He turns to her and smiles. Sure, he says,
he'll read. He'd meant before, I now remember, that the books
she'd brought were all too old for her, but he's
agreed to read one anyway, "out loud." That way, he
explains, it lasts a longer time. So when she asks
"Is it too old?" she means of course "for someone of my age."
But he's persuaded by this point and opens Bronte,
does the whole Chautauqua for the sister-boy on his knee.
In Salt Lake City J.B. said: Matthias, don't

[374]

read Proust until you're over forty—and so of course I started it
at once, looking, as we do, for secrets someone
thinks we shouldn't yet be privy to.

So there it ends in the selva oscura with *Wuthering Heights*,
the wardens having left the store & on their trail.
Which means he couldn't finish it, or was it really done?
Nights when I'm afraid and cannot sleep, Diana often says
Then shall I read? She means of course "out loud."
She knows that way it lasts a longer time. I always ask
for something that's too young for me, more likely
Pathfinder than Proust. It's what we have invented to
shut down my fear, send me off onto some quiet lake of peace.
She'll say, Some boy's adventure maybe?
How about your macho friend E.H.?
And I'll say, Adams, that's not fair! But I end up with
what I liked the best when I was twelve, & that was Adams
fishing here in Michigan. We don't do Heathcliff at Chautauqua;
we just troll on out for my one bass.

Although right now, awake, the outboard dead,
we do not have a line or pole or net.
You don't get bass or trout or marlin with your mind alone
(even if it conjures tigers in your bed).
We sit here rocking in the shallows, drinking wine.
The naked girls are gone. Shadows fall across
the party on the lawn. I am content.
But that's what Faust says when he's done for,
when he gazes on his works of reclamation in the hands of
that Chautauqua in apotheosis, old Herr G.
So things can be too Swell for our own good, swell
out of hand, grow cosmic in their folding
space right over into time. It's just the wine, my love,

the rocking on these waves, and it will pass.
This started out to be a poem about a bass I caught when
I was ten. And never once again.
You'll read to me tonight, I know. Whether Proust or
Mother Goose, it does its work. It's no big show
at the Chautauqua with a smell of gaslight, but it's exactly swell
enough, no more. It's great. In my life it's starting to get late.
We haven't yet found Windemere
and now the sun has set entirely on the lake.

Afterword

I have made selections of my work twice before. *Northern Summer* was published in England and America in 1984. It included both short and longer poems and was intended to be fairly inclusive, running to more than two hundred pages. That length allowed me to include, along with the title poem, all of *The Stefan Bathory Poems* and a substantial selection of *The Mihail Lermontov Poems*. I did not include any of the long poems from *Bucyrus*, my first book. A decade later I made a different kind of selection in a volume published only in America, *Swimming at Midnight*. All long poems were printed in a companion volume, *Beltane at Aphelion*, leaving me free to publish what I had never published before, a book of exclusively short and middle-length poems.

For a poet working both in longer and shorter forms, selections are always difficult. Poets as different as Auden and Rexroth have also resorted to dividing longer and shorter poems in separate volumes. The problem, of course, is that only one reader out of a hundred will ever acquire a separate and usually expensive volume of longer poems, however much he or she may be tempted to do so by some of the shorter work. My experience with *Swimming at Midnight* and *Beltane at Aphelion* was instructive; *Swimming* sold out its first printing almost immediately and *Beltane*, available only in cloth, sold very few copies indeed. The fact that only the shorter poems were published in paper probably suggests that the publisher felt that the longer poems were mainly destined for libraries. At any rate, I am now trying once again to integrate shorter and longer poems in a single volume, hoping that a reader of short poems will also become a reader of longer ones.

But there is of course another problem. When I made the selections for *Northern Summer*, I had before me twenty years of work. I now have before me forty years of work. So if I am to include longer poems, or at least substantial selections from longer poems, a good deal will need to be left out. It is easy enough to put aside once more the long poems from *Bucyrus*. It also makes sense to exclude the two long poems recently published by Salt in *Working Progress, Working Title*, as they are still very much available in a separate volume. Among other longer poems, the *Bathory* and *Lermontov* cycles seem to have dated, so this time I am omitting these. But all of the omissions are made chiefly in order to admit almost all of *A Gathering of Ways*, the three long poems published in America in 1991 which have never been printed in Britain. I have decided, in violation of chronology, to print "Facts From an Apocryphal Midwest" in section I of the present volume, along with a few shorter poems and excerpts written twenty years and more before I began work on *A Gathering*. The poem, I hope, establishes the American Midwest as indeed a home, however much many of the poems that follow may be in search of another. For fifteen years I wrote only when I was living in England, usually in Cambridge or at my wife's home in Suffolk during summers and academic leaves when I was free of most ordinary obligations and therefore able to concentrate fully on writing poems. For years I felt I had to explain this to American readers, especially as many of the poems had British subjects or contexts and because East Anglia had become deeply important as a place that had changed me as a person and led to the composition of many poems I would never have written had I not lived there. But what I thought of for a while as a way of life—teaching in America, but writing always in England—turned out in fact to be a phase, and my work eventually returned, as I did myself, to the American Midwest where it began in 1963 with "Swimming at Midnight." The essential frame of this book is intended to be "Facts From an Apocryphal Midwest" and "Swell," the cycle that concludes the volume and is set at Walloon Lake in Michigan.

The other two sections from *A Gathering of Ways*, "An East Anglian Diptych" and most of "A Compostela Diptych," fit comfortably enough, respectively, at the conclusion of section III and, all alone because of its substantial length, even in excerpts, as section VI. "An East Anglian Diptych" makes sense as a kind of resolution to a section of poems dealing in various ways with historical, geographical, topological and cultural matters taken up in work that was written mainly in Suffolk and Cambridge during the 1970s and early 80s. The Compostela poem ranges farther afield. It derives from the summer of 1987 when I walked parts of the Via Tolosana pilgrimage route over Somport Pass and on through Jaca, San Juan de la Peña, Leyre, Sanguesa, Pamplona, Puente la Reina, Estella, Logroño, Najera, Santo Domingo de la Calzada, and Burgos, crossing back into France through the pass at

Roncesvalles. Having written two poems where I felt on very familiar ground—though in two different ways—I began here to explore a ground with which I was totally unfamiliar, except through the literature to which it had given birth from the troubadours to Walter Starkie and Eleanor Munro. At any rate, the three parts of *A Gathering of Ways* are all represented here, though separated by shorter and middle-length poems along the way.

The rest of the book is easy to describe. Sections II and III include short and middle length poems from *Turns* (1975), *Crossing* (1979), and the last section of *Northern Summer* (1984). The order is not strictly chronological, though only "An East Anglian Diptych," inserted at the end of III from the volume of 1991 mentioned above, was written after 1983. Section IV includes a few more short poems from the end of *Northern Summer* and a group of what were "New Poems" when *Swimming at Midnight* was published in 1995. The section concludes with the "Northern Summer" cycle itself, looking back at a period spent in Fife at the Wemyss Castle Estate in 1980 after our family had lost the house in Suffolk. Section V is mainly a selection of recent poems about poetry, writing, mapping and collecting. It begins with two translations and concludes with excerpts from the long poem "Cuttings" which appeared in *Pages* (2000). Section VI, as mentioned before, contains most of "A Compostela Diptych," while section VII is a group of previously unpublished poems, two more selections from *Swimming at Midnight*, some shorter poems from *Pages*, and "Swell," published as a chapbook in 2002. When I began considering the contents for this book, I was only certain of two things: that each section should end with a longer poem or excerpts from a longer poem, and that the volume as a whole should conclude with "Swell." I think the reader will see that it could scarcely conclude with anything else.

Notes

Jules Michelet, *Satanism and Witchcraft* ("Renaissance"); Julio Caro Baroja, *The World of the Witches* in the Glendinning translation, from which several phrases are quoted & paraphrased ("An Absence"). John Read, *Prelude to Chemistry*; Frederic Spiegleberg, *Alchemy as a Way of Salvation*; C.G. Jung, "The Idea of Redemption in Alchemy" ("Five Lyrics from 'Poem in Three Parts'"); Christopher Caudwell, *The Concept of Freedom*, from which the long quote is taken ("Statement").

"Facts From An Apocryphal Midwest." Like "An East Anglian Diptych" (p. 145 ff.), this poem deals with trails and rivers. The chief trails here began as prehistoric paths down which Lake Superior copper was carried from the early days of the Mound Builders until the collapse of their particular economy and way of life. These trails, and especially the Old Sauk Trail and the St. Joseph-Kankakee portage, were later used by the Potawatomi, the Miami and other local Algonquian tribes, as well as by the Iroquois on their raids into the area, and by the French explorers, traders and missionaries. As in the East Anglian poem, three rivers figure in the topographical configuration that emerges: the St. Joseph (which the French called the River of Miamis), the Kankakee (also called the Seignelay), and the Illinois. The dominant historical figure in the poem is Réné-Robert Cavelier, Sieur de La Salle. Returning to Indiana after a period of living and writing in East Anglia, I found myself stimulated by exactly those things which from time to time I had thought might stimulate "another poet" — La Salle's voyage through the great lakes and journey along the local paths and waterways, Algonquian (mostly Potawatomi) history and mythology, the geological and geographical transformations which occurred during the last glacial recession, and the prose of Francis Parkman in the volume of *France and England in North America* called *La Salle and the Discovery of the Great West*. Although I do not take La Salle all the way to the Mississippi (usually called the Colbert in the poem), I take him pretty far down the Illinois. For some of the same reasons that Edward Thomas and John Constable appear in "An East Anglian Diptych," Parkman himself appears briefly here. His prose is sometimes quoted, paraphrased, versified. Where quotations are not exact, I intend no disrespect. Formal constraints now and then demanded slight modifications in rhythm, diction and syntax. Neither Fenimore Cooper's stagecoach ride into the area nor the dedication of the LaSalle Memorial Project are fictions. The merging of the two, however, in the context of a pageant which occurred at the quatro-millennial anniversary of the La Salle-Miami Council is only a convenient way, consistent with the conclusion of both "Ley Lines" and "Rivers" in "An East Anglian Diptych," to bring the poem into the present historical period.

Among the sources for this poem are three that very few readers will have come across. These are books by an almost vanished breed, the local amateur historian. Charles H. Bartlett's *La Salle in the Valley of the St. Joseph*, George A. Baker's *The St. Joseph-Kankakee Portage*, and Timothy Edward Howard's *A History of St. Joseph County* were all enormously useful. Other sources for the poem include: Charles Haight Farnham, *A Life of Francis Parkman*; Howard Doughty, *Francis Parkman*; Louise Phelps Kellogg, *Early Narratives of the Northwest* and *The French Regime in Wisconsin and the Northwest*; Henri Joutel, *A Journal of La Salle's Last Voyage*; Carl O. Sauer, *Seventeenth Century North America* and *Selected Essays 1963–1975*; James A. Clifton, *The Prairie People*; R. David Edmunds, *The Potawatomis*; George T. Hunt, *The Wars of the Iroquois*; Fay Folsom Nichols, *The Kankakee*; Archer Butler Hulbert, *Indian Thoroughfares*; Hugh Brody, *Maps and Dreams*; Andrew Trout, *Jean-Baptiste Colbert*; James Fenimore Cooper, *The Oak Openings: or The Bee Hunter*; George Dekker, *James Fenimore Cooper: The American Scott*; Blake Nevius, *Cooper's Landscapes: An Essay on the Picturesque Vision*.

PART II

Tags from Yeats, Joyce, de Sade, Octavio Paz, Marianne Moore, and Jean Cocteau ("For John, After His Visit"). F.S. Howes, *The English Musical Renaissance* ("Once For English Music"). Edmund Wilson, *To the Finland Station* ("Three Around a Revolution"). Paul Hindemith, *Libretto: Matis der Maler*; Otto Benesch, *The Art of the Renaissance in Northern Europe*, chapter II; Ian Kemp, *Hindemith*; F.W. Sternfeld, ed., *Music in the Modern Age*, chapter 2: "Germany", Elaine Padmore; Norman Cohn, *The Pursuit of the Millennium* ("Double Sonnet on the Absence of Text: 'Symphony Matis der Maler', Berlin, 1934:—Metamorphoses"). Thomas Hardy, *Jude the Obscure*; H.T. Lowe Porter, translator's note, *Dr. Faustus*; A.F.E. Burroughs, *West Midland Dialects of the Fourteenth Century*; J. Matthias, *Bucyrus* and "Th'Entencioun and Speche of Philosophers"; tags from King Alfred, Chaucer, Langland, John of Mandeville, Wycliffe, the *Pearl* poet, Joseph of Arimathaea; George Steiner, *Language and Silence* ("Turns"). *The Great Tournament Roll of Westminster, A Collotype Reproduction of the Manuscript*: Sidney Anglo's Historical Introduction, Appendices I and II—Tiptoft's Ordinances and the Revels Account of Richard Gibson, and the Analytical Description; Gordon Donaldson, *Scottish Kings*; Lt.Colonel Howard Green, *Battlefields of Britain and Ireland*; Peter Alexander, Introduction to Shakespeare's (?) *Henry VIII* in the Collins Tudor Shakespeare ("Double Derivation, Association, & Cliché: from *The Great Tournament Roll of Westminster*"). Thomas Nashe, "A Litany in Time of Plague" ("Clarifications for Robert Jacoby"). Johan Huizinga, *Homo Ludens: The Manual of Horsemanship of the British Horse Society and Pony Club*; Lars Norén, "August"; tags from John Berryman, W.B. Yeats, Robert Hass, Wordsworth, *King Lear* ("Poem for Cynouai").

PART III

Bryan Houghton, *Saint Edmund, King and Martyr* ("Double Invocation . . . "); Enid Porter, *The Folklore of East Anglia* ("The Fen Birds' Cry"); C.J. Stranks, *St. Etheldreda: Queen and Abbas*; *The Book of Margery Kempe* (translated by W. Butler-Bowdon with an introduction by R.W. Chambers); Julian of Norwich, *Revelations of Divine Love* (in the Clifton Wolters translation); P. Franklin Chambers, *Juliana of Norwich: an Introductory Appreciation and an Interpretive Anthology* ("Two Ladies" and "59 Lines Assembled Quickly Sitting on a Wall Near the Reconstruction of the Lady Juliana's Cell"). Justin Kaplan, *Mr. Clemens and Mark Twain*; Mark Twain, "The Celebrated

Jumping Frog of Calavaras County" ("Mark Twain in the Fens"). Joanna Richardson, *Verlaine*; Enid Starkie, *Arthur Rimbaud*; Paul Verlaine, "Sagesse" ("Paul Verlaine in Lincolnshire"). Sir Geoffrey Keynes, ed., *Sir Thomas Browne: Selected Writings* ("Words for Sir Thomas Browne"). W.G. Arnott, *Orwell Estuary*; George Ewart Evans, *Ask the Fellows Who Cut the Hay*; Julia Pipe, *Port on the Alde*; Rudyard Kipling, "A Smuggler's Song" ("Lines for the Gentlemen"). César Vallejo, "Ágape" from *Los Heraldos Negros* ("Agape"). Julian Tennyson, *Suffolk Scene* ("Brandon, Breckland: The Flint Knappers"). R.A. Edwards, *The Fighting Bishop*; R.B. Dobson, ed., *The Peasants' Revolt of 1381*; Rodney Hilton, *Bond Men Made Free*; Norman Cohn, *The Pursuit of the Millennium* ("26 June 1381/1977").

"An East Anglian Diptych." This is very much a "poem of place" located in those parts of Cambridgeshire, Suffolk and Norfolk linked by the ley lines and rivers which connect locality with locality and time with time. The ley lines in question are the ancient paths and tracks which date back to the Neolithic period. The chief ley line followed is the Icknield Way, the track explored by Edward Thomas in his final volume of prose on the English countryside. Thomas himself figures in the prose section of the first part of the sequence, section iv. The controlling myth for both "Ley Lines" and "Rivers" derives from T.C. Lethbridge's *Gogmagog: The Buried Gods*, which treats the old Celtic/Belgic religion in terms of his excavation of the Wandelbury chalk figures and their relationship to better known hill figures such as the Cerne Giant. The presiding presences in "Ley Lines" (who also return in "Rivers") are the dowser—Lethbridge himself was a dowser— and his prototype, the Dodman, who was the prehistoric surveyor who aligned the paths and tracks. The transition between the "Ley Lines" section and the "Rivers" is made by way of the terrestrial zodiac at Bury St. Edmund's, a vast arrangement of figures by means of which I move from the Sagittarius beginning on the River Lark near Abbots Bridge in Bury to the Gemini (in the form of Wandil, the East Anglian devil) standing on the Stour near Clare Castle. The rivers dealt with are, in order, the Stour, the Alde, and the Deben. As in "Ley Lines," this section shuttles backwards and forwards in time, though its geographical or topological movement is direct enough. This part too has a section in prose, John Constable on the Stour corresponding to Edward Thomas on the Icknield Way. The gods and goddesses invoked in both sections are the same: Gog (the sun/Bel/Baal/Belenus/Helith, etc.), Magog (the moon/Meg/Magg/Epona, etc.), and Wandil (darkness /the East Anglian devil/the giant with a sword, etc.). When the last section of "Ley Lines" moves into the present by counting off the numbers which locate Whittlesford church on the Ordnance Survey Map, the fit of alliteration is not gratuitous. The Shiela-na-gig figure over the Whittlesford church door is an image of Gogmagog, and Lethbridge argues that words like "goggle," "giggle," "ogle," and the child's grotesque toy "Golliwog" are all verbal derivations. The end of "Rivers," like the end of "Ley Lines," also moves into the present—but without the fit of alliteration.

Sources: T.C. Lethbridge, *GogMagog*; Shirley Toulson, *East Anglia: Walking the Ley Lines and Ancient Tracks*; W.G. Arnott, *Alde Estuary*, *Orwell Estuary: The Story of Ipswich River*, *Suffolk Estuary: The Story of the River Deben*; George Ewart Evans, *The Pattern Under the Plough*, *Ask the Fellows Who Cut the Hay*; Julia Pipe, *Port on the Alde*; R. Allen

Brown, *Orford Castle*; F.J.E. Raby and P.K. Baillie Reynolds, *Framlingham Castle*; O.R. Sitwell, *Framlingham Guide*; Julian Tennyson, *Suffolk Scene*; Rupert Bruce-Mitford, *The Sutton Hoo Ship Burial*; Bernice Grohskopf, *The Treasure of Sutton Hoo*; Michael Alexander, trans., *Beowulf*; W.J. Ashley, ed., *Edward III and His Wars, 1327–1360*; Michael Prestwich, *The Three Edwards*; William Longman, *The Life and Times of Edward the Third*.

PART IV

Grimm's Fairy Tales, trans. Margaret Hunt with an introduction by Frances Clarke Sayers ("Not Having Heard a Single Fairy Tale"). Richard Burns, *The Manager*; Branko Miljković, "While You Are Singing" ("Public Poem"). Ezra Pound, "Cino" ("E.P. in Crawfordsville"). Arthur Mizner, *The Saddest Story* ("F.M.F. from Olivet"). Sir John Rothenstein, *Modern British Painters*, Vols. 1, 2, and 3 ("Mr. Rothenstein's Rudiments"). Osip Mandelstam, "Lines on Stalin"; Nadezhda Mandelstam, *Hope Against Hope* ("Horace Augustus Mandelstam Stalin"). "Friendship," reprinted in the present book, was translated into Serbian by Ivan Lalic; the Serbian word in the first line is the title of the poem; the other Serbian words are my Christian name and surname ("Into Cyrillic"). Oto Bihalji-Merin and Alojz Benac, *Bogomil Sculpture*; Jacques Lacarriere, *The Gnostics* ("Bogomil in Languedoc" and "The Silence of Stones"). François Villon, "L'Epitaphe Villon"; Mrs. Thatcher on The Falklands, quoted in *Le Monde*; Neil Lands, *The French Pyrenees*; E. Cortade, *Collioure: Guide Historique et Touristique*; Yves Bonnefoy, "Jean et Jeanne"; Antonio Machado, "El sol es un globo de fuego"; Guiraud Riquièr, "Be'm degra de chantar tener . . . "; Stéphane Mallarmé," "Prose—Pour des Esseintes" ("A Wind in Roussillon"). Sir William Fraser, *Memorials of the Family of Wemyss of Wemyss*; Göran Sonnevi, "Void which falls out of void . . . "; *The Gododdin*; Antonia Fraser, *Mary Queen of Scots*; Robert Gore-Brown, *Lord Bothwell and Mary Queen of Scots*; Moray McLaren, *Bonnie Prince Charlie*; John Prebble, *Culloden*; Sir Walter Scott, *Waverley*; Robert Louis Stevenson, *Kidnapped*; Jenni Calder, *Robert Louis Stevenson*; A.N. Wilson, *The Laird of Abbotsford*; Adam Smith, *The Wealth of Nations*; Fred R. Glahe, *Adam Smith and the Wealth of Nations*; R.B. Haldane, *Adam Smith*; E.W. Hirst, *Adam Smith*; John Rae, *The Life of Adam Smith*; John Fleming, *Robert Adam and His Circle*; James Macpherson, *The Poems of Ossian*; Derick S. Thomson, *The Gaelic Sources of MacPherson's Ossian*; Baily Saunders, *Life and Letters of James Macpherson*; Henry Mackenzie, *The Man of Feeling*; Gerard A. Barker, *Henry Mackenzie* ("Northern Summer").

PART V

Branko Miljković, "Dok Budeš Pevao" ("While You Are Singing"). Göran Sonnevi, "Tomrum som faller . . ." from *Ingrepp-modeller* ("Void which falls out of void . . ."). Robert Hass, "Letter to a Poet" and other poems from *Field Guide* ("On Rereading a Friend's First Book"). Blaise Cendrars, *Complete Poems*, trans. by Ron Padgett; Federico Garcia Lorca, *Poet in New York*, trans. Greg Simon and Steven F. White ("Two in New York" and "Easter 1912 and Christmas 1929 . . ."). Edward Rice, *Captain Sir Richard Francis Burton*; Charles Nicholl, *Somebody Else: Arthur Rimbaud in Africa*; Arthur Rimbaud, *Complete Works*, trans. Paul Schmidt ("Two in Harar").

Gertrude Bell, *The Desert and the Sown*; Janet Wallach, *Desert Queen* ("She Maps Iraq"). Anna Akhmatova, *My Half Century: Selected Prose*; Roberta Reeder, *Anna Akhmatova: Poet and Prophet* ("Six or So in Petersburg"); René Char, *Fureur et Mystère, Feuillets d'Hypnos*; Carrie Noland, *Poetry at Stake* ("Francophiles, 1958").

From "Cuttings." Like the sequence as a whole, these excerpted parts draw directly, without external attribution, from a wide range of poems, letters, journals, and scientific literatures of the 18th and early 19th centuries, as well as from contemporary scholarly and critical sources. From the original Part III, "Endeavors" 1–5: Wilfred Blunt, *The Art of Botanical Illustration*; Jean-Jacques Rousseau, *Letters on the Elements of Botany Addressed to a Lady*; C.E. Vulliamy, *Rousseau*; William H. Blanchard, *Rousseau and the Spirit of Revolt*; Robert John Thornton, *The Temple of Flora*; Hugh Macmillan, *The Poetry of Plants*; John Ruskin, *Proserpina*; John Dixon Hunt, *The Wider Sea: A Life of John Ruskin*; Alan Bewell, *Jacobin Plants: Botany as Social Theory in the 1790s*; Mary Louise Pratt, *Imperial Eyes: Travel Writing and Transculturation*; Judith Pascoe, *Female Botanists and the Poetry of Charlotte Smith*; Kenneth Lemmon, *The Golden Age of Plant Hunters*; Percy Bysshe Shelley, "The Sensitive Plant." From the original Part II, "As Kew As You": Ronald King, *Royal Kew*; Richard Mabey, *The Flowers of Kew*; The Rev. W. Mason, "Heroic Epistle to Sir William Chambers"; Erasmus Darwin, "Botanic Garden"; Stephen Duck, "The Thresher's Labour"; Thomas Chatterton, "Kew Gardens"; Fanny Burney, the Diaries and the Letters; Wilfrid Blunt, *The Art of Botanical Illustration*; Gordon Dunthorne, *Flower and Fruit Prints of the 18th and Early 19th Centuries*.

Part VI

"A Compostela Diptych." As with the two earlier long poems that between the summer of 1984 and the winter of 1990 slowly took their place in a trilogy—"Facts From an Apocryphal Midwest" (p. 16 ff.) and "An East Anglian Diptych" (p. 145 ff.)— I have more debts here than I can possibly acknowledge. Stylistically, David Jones is once again a welcome and benevolent presence. Indeed his good help and hope have actually become, in a sense, one of the subjects of the present poem. The same could be said of Ezra Pound up through the walk from Excideuil. I have leaned heavily on a number of translations. Although the poet knows the various languages which he must sometimes quote all too imperfectly himself, the poem's polylingual texture is essential: it is necessary for the reader to try and hear the Latin, French, Spanish and Provençal words as best he can. I need particularly to acknowledge W.S. Merwin's translation of the *Poema del Cid*, Robert Harrison's and Dorothy L. Sayers' translations of the *Chanson de Roland*, and the three translations, one into French and two into English, of the Pilgrim's Guide attributed to Aimery Picaud from the *Codex Calixtinus* listed below with my full range of sources. Walter Starkie's *The Road to Santiago*, Roman Menéndez Pidal's *The Cid and His Spain*, and Eleanor Munro's *On Glory Roads* have been my constant companions. (Much in Part I derives from Munro's interpretation of the visual setting and internal structures of pilgrimage in the light of archaeo- and ethno-astronomical theory.) Occasional phrases from these books turn up in the poem itself, as also from the texts by Meyer Shapiro, Erwin Panofsky, Umberto Eco, Jules Michelet, Thomas Carlyle, Desmond Seward, Jacques Lacarriere, Emmanuel Le Roy Ladurie, Henry

Chadwick, Alphonsus M. Liguori, Edward Peters, John James, Jan Read, J.A. Condé, Oleg Grabar, Henry Kamen, Christopher Hibbert, Franz Cumont, Henry Sedgwick, Johan Huizinga, Bruno S. James, Edgar Holt and Adam Nicholson listed below. Borrowings in the poem are usually indicated by italics.

Sources for Part I: Jeanne Vielliard, *Guide De Pèlerin de Saint-Jacques de Compostelle* (Texte Latin du XIIe Siècle, Édité et Traduit en Francais d'Après Les Manuscripts de Compostelle et de Ripoll); Constantine Christofides, *Notes Toward a History of Medieval and Renaissance Art, with a Translation of 'The Pilgrim's Guide to Saint-James of Compostela'*; Paula L. Gerson, Annie Shaver-Crandall, & M. Alison Stones, eds. & translators, *Pilgrims' Guide to Santiago de Compostela*; A. Kingsley Porter, *Romanesque Sculpture of the Pilgrimage Roads*; Meyer Sharpiro, *Romanesque Art*; Joseph Gantner, *The Glory of Romanesque Art*; Vera Hell, *The Great Pilgrimage of the Middle Ages*; Eusebio Goicoechea Arrondo, *The Way to Santiago*; *El Camino de Santiago: Guia Del Peregrino*; Eleanor Munro, *On Glory Roads: A Pilgrim's Book about Pilgrimage*; Walter Starkie, *The Road to Santiago*; Noreen Hunt, *Cluniac Monasticism in the Central Middle Ages, Cluny Under Saint Hugh 1049–1109*; Jacobus de Voragine, *The Golden Legend* (translated and adapted from the Latin by Granger Ryan and Helmut Ripperger); Christopher Page, *Voices and Instruments of the Middle Ages: Instrumental Practice and Songs in France 1100–1300*; Russell Chamberlin, *The Emperor Charlemagne*; Charles Edward Russell, *Charlemagne: First of the Moderns*; Peter Munz, *Life in the Age of Charlemagne*; H.R. Loyn and John Percival, *The Reign of Charlemagne: Documents on Carolingian Government and Administration*; H.W. Garrod and R.B. Mowat, eds., *Einhard's Life of Charlemagne*; Robert Harrison, trans., *The Song of Roland*; Dorothy L. Sayers, trans., *The Song of Roland*; Edward Peters, *Heresy and Authority in Medieval Europe*; Msgr. Leon Cristiani, *Heresies and Heretics*; St. Alphonsus M. Liguori, *The History of Heresies, and their refutation* (trans. from the Italian by the Rev. John T. Mullock); Henry Chadwick, *Priscillian of Avila*; Jacques Lacarriere, *The Gnostics*; Emmanuel Le Roy Ladurie, *Montaillou: The Promised Land of Error*; Joseph R. Strayer, *The Albigensian Crusades*; Desmond Seward, *Eleanor of Aquitaine: The Mother Queen*; Johan Huizinga, *The Waning of the Middle Ages*; Peter Makin, *Provence and Pound*; Adam Nicholson, *Long Walks in France*. Sources for "Intercalation": Erwin Panofsky, ed. and trans., *Abbot Suger on the Abbey Church of St.-Denis and Its Art Treasures*; Umberto Eco, *Art and Beauty in the Middle Ages*; Bruno S. James, *Saint Bernard of Clairvaux*; Donald Francis Firebaugh, *St. Bernard's Preaching of the Second Crusade*; Thomas Merton, *The Last of the Fathers*; Henry Adams, *Mont-Saint-Michel and Chartres*; Steven Runciman, *A History of the Crusades*; Odo of Deuil, *De Profectione Ludovici VII in Orientem*; John Hugh Hill and Laurita Lyttleton Hill, *Raymond IV Count of Toulouse*; Jules Michelet, *History of the French Revolution*, Vol. VII (Books 14–17), trans. by Keith Botsford; Thomas Carlyle, *The French Revolution*; John James, *The Traveller's Key to Medieval France: A Guide to the Sacred Architecture of Medieval France*. Sources for Part II: J.A. Condé, *History of the Dominion of the Arabs in Spain*; Jan Read, *The Moors in Spain and Portugal*; Oleg Grabar, *The Formation of Islamic Art*; Keith Albarn, Jenny Miall Smith, Stanford Steele, Diana Walker, *The Language of Pattern*; W.S. Merwin, trans. *The Poem of the Cid* (with facing page Spanish text of the edition of Ramon Menéndez Pidal), *From the Spanish Morning: Translations of Spanish Ballads*; Ramon Menéndez Pidal, *The Cid and His Spain*, *Poesia Juglaresca y Origenes de las Literaturas Romancias*; Ernest Merimée and S. Griswold Morley, *A History of Spanish Literature*;

David William Foster, *The Early Spanish Ballad*; Cecil Roth, *The Spanish Inquisition*; Henry Kamen, *The Spanish Inquisition*; David Gates, *The Spanish Ulcer: A History of the Peninsular War*; Richard Humble, *Napoleon's Peninsular Marshals*; Christopher Hibbert, *Corunna*; W. H. Fitchett, ed., *Wellington's Men: Some Soldier Autobiographies*; C.S. Forester, *The Gun*, Hugh Thomas, *The Spanish Civil War*; Franz Cumont, *The Mysteries of Mithra*; M.J. Vermaseren, *Mithras: The Secret God*; Francisco Goya, *The Complete Etchings, Aquatints and Lithographs*; Eleanor Elsner, *The Romance of the Basque Country and the Pyrenees*; Johnannes Jorgensen, *St. Francis of Assisi*; Omer Englebert, *Saint Francis of Assisi*; Henry Dwight Sedgwick, *Ignatius Loyola*; Mary Purcell, *The First Jesuit*; Walter Nigg, *Warriors of God: The Great Religious Orders and their Founders*; W.S. Porter, *Early Spanish Monasticism*; Edgar Holt, *The Carlist Wars in Spain*.

PART VII

The poems about music and composers in this section derive chiefly from the compositions themselves, the multi-volume *Grove Dictionary of Music*, *The Harvard Dictionary of Music*, CD liner notes, and the standard biographies. I should be more specific with regard to the poem on Arnold Schoenberg: Willi Reich, *Schoenberg: A Critical Biography*; H.H. Stuckenschmidt, *Arnold Schoenberg*; Alexander L. Ringer, *Arnold Schoenberg: The Composer as Jew*; Pamela Cooper-White, *Schoenberg and the God-Idea: The Opera "Moses und Aron"*; Thomas Mann, *Doctor Faustus*; Gunilla Bergsten, *Thomas Mann's "Doctor Faustus": The Sources and Structure of the Novel* ("Diminished Third"). "Master Class" derives from Lotte Lehmann's *Eighteen Song Cycles: Studies in Their Interpretation*. The section on Schubert in "Unfinished" derives from Christopher H. Gibbs's *The Life of Schubert*; those on Haydn's last quartets and Shostakovich's *The Gamblers* from liner notes to the Sony and BMG recordings. The remaining list of sources pertain to the poems not concerned with music. Walter Arndt, ed. and trans., *Alexander Pushkin: Collected Narrative and Lyrical Poetry*; Neal Ascherson, *Black Sea*; Peter Green, trans., *Ovid: The Poems of Exile*; Clarence Brown and W.S. Merwin, trans., *Osip Mandelstam, "Tristia"*; Yon Barna, *Eisenstein* ("Sadnesses: Black Seas"). Christopher Bamford, ed., *The Noble Traveller: The Life and Writings of O.V. de L. Milosz*; John Peck, trans., O.V. de L. Milosz, "Quand Elle Viendra . . . " ("Geneva Pension").Wilbur F. Hinman, *The Story of the Sherman Brigade* ("Ohio Forbears"). Peter Jay, trans., *The Song of Songs* ("Variations on The Song of Songs"); William Carlos Williams, "The Turtle" ("Letter to an Unborn Grandson"); Ernest Hemingway, the novels and stories; Michael Reynolds, the five volumes of his Hemingway biography; Constance Cappel, *Hemingway in Michigan*; Dorothy Munson Krenrich, *Muhqua Nebis: Legends of Walloon Lake* ("Swell").

3 5282 00580 0712

Printed in the United Kingdom
by Lightning Source UK Ltd.
101643UKS00001B/379-381